CLOSER to JESUS

CLOSER to JESUS

▸ 5-Minute Devotions
for Living and Loving
Like Christ

Alexis Waid

ROCKRIDGE
PRESS

Copyright © 2022 by Rockridge Press

First Rockridge Press trade paperback edition 2022

Rockridge Press and the Rockridge Press logo are trademarks or registered trademarks of Callisto Media Inc. and/or its affiliates in the United States and other countries and may not be used without written permission.

For general information on our other products and services, please contact our Customer Care Department within the United States at (866) 744-2665, or outside the United States at (510) 253-0500.

Paperback ISBN: 978-1-68539-646-6 | eBook ISBN: 978-1-68539-817-0

Manufactured in the United States of America

Art Producer: Janice Ackerman
Editor: Mo Mozuch
Production Manager: Jose Olivera

Photography © Vovik Mar/iStock, cover and pp. ii-iii; All other images used under license from Shutterstock.

10 9 8 7 6 5 4 3 2 1 0

Dedicated to the many Christian authors, thinkers, theologians, and servants of Christ over the past 2,000 years who have shaped me with their faith.

Contents

PART 2: LOVE LIKE JESUS   41

PART 3: LOOK TO JESUS 81

Introduction

I couldn't be more excited to present this devotional book that will provide you with impactful opportunities to curate five minutes with Jesus every day. My name is Alexis, and I have been a follower of Jesus since 1999. I have worked in ministry since 2004, and my heart yearns to help people grow closer to God and His likeness. My life has radically changed, and it continually changes, because of Jesus and His immense guidance in my life. Jesus—and His love and truth—has altered who I am, and He continues to grow me and heal me.

What excites me most about this devotional is that it gives you a well-rounded picture of Jesus in ways you may not have encountered before. There is so much to learn from our Lord, and I believe He has much in store for you through this devotional.

We can never spend enough time with Jesus. There is always more He can teach us as we travel on our journey with God. The fruit that comes from spending time with Jesus is the same fruit that Paul speaks of in Galatians 5:22–23: love, joy, peace, patience, kindness, goodness, faithfulness, gentleness, and self-control. These attributes, which are known as the fruit of the Spirit, are just a few of many markers of a growing and flourishing follower of Jesus and His way.

Jesus grows and sustains these holy virtues in us through our time spent with Him. The more we invest in our relationship with Jesus, the more these attributes will grow.

This book will take you through the scope of Jesus's ministerial life, giving you glimpses in five-minute doses that will enable you to see Jesus more in depth. This book aims to help you understand Jesus—the real person who is at the same time our God. It's vital to understand Jesus because His life and ministry are an example for all of us. He shows us how to deal with adversity, how to cope with loss, how to have hope and belief in the future, how to have endless strength and fortitude in our troubles, what real pure love looks like, and how to treat others and treat ourselves, just to name a few examples. There isn't a scenario in life that Jesus cannot reach.

Often, when we look at Jesus, we focus intently on His miracles and other attention-grabbing stories. Although we will certainly traverse those profound and powerful stories, we will also look at the often-surprising in-between moments when Jesus shows us who He is and how He interacts with others, which teach us valuable lessons for our own lives and our relationships with others. Throughout this devotional, you will get an immersive experience of what it looks like to be with Jesus in new ways and allow Him to directly impact your life.

How to Use This Devotional

This devotional is organized into three sections:

Part 1: Live Like Jesus   **Part 3:** Look to Jesus

Part 2: Love Like Jesus

Part 1 invites you into the life of Jesus, the way He did things, the impact of His life, and how His message provides comfort and strength for your life.

Part 2 focuses on Jesus's examples of love, especially the way He loved others and the love He has for you.

Part 3 examines current pressures and problems every Christian faces, what Jesus has to say about those pressures and problems, and how He can lead you through them.

Each part has thirty-eight devotions that include a title, Bible verse, commentary, and rotating bonus feature. Each devotion will take just five minutes to complete. Although the devotions are short, they are all designed to be powerful and impactful for your life.

The pace of this devotional is up to you. Whether you enjoy mornings, afternoons, evenings, or miscellaneous times, feel free to create your own pace, setting, and timetable. In addition, it might be beneficial for you to accompany the devotion with a journal because some of the bonus features call for journaling exercises.

All scriptures quoted in this devotional are from the New International Version (NIV). The NIV is a standard and easy-to-use translation, but please feel free to use whichever translation best suits you.

Taking the Time to Strengthen Your Bond with Jesus

As followers of Jesus, it's so important to spend time with Him. This devotional will help you connect with our Savior five minutes at a time, to hear His truth, learn His way, and find your answers in Him.

By living with, loving, and looking to Jesus, you will get a robust picture of the life of Jesus and how He is calling you in your own life. There is so much value in examining Jesus; He is an endless pool of refreshment for our souls and encouragement for our journey.

I'm excited to begin this journey with you. I am confident that along the way Jesus will show you new and invigorating things about Himself. He will tend to you in the precise ways that you need, and He will lead you closer to Him and His likeness, helping you bear much fruit. It's going to be a very good journey indeed.

PART 1

▶ LIVE LIKE JESUS

Jesus's ministerial life, which is primarily captured in the four Gospels—Matthew, Mark, Luke, and John—offers a snapshot of how Jesus responded to strangers, friends, oppressors, religious leaders, pariahs, and His followers. As Jesus interacted with others, He did extraordinary things, performing miracles and healings and offering profound teachings. Jesus's radical and powerful teachings then were unlike anything anyone had ever experienced, and they still hold the same profound power today. In this section, we will explore Jesus's life and teaching in ways that translate directly to your everyday life. It is my hope that Jesus will become more tangible for you and that you will begin to find more commonality with Him than you ever have before. For Jesus is the way, He is our hope, and He shows us, through Him, a whole new way to live life. Let's jump right in and see where He takes us!

SEEK JESUS

*But seek first his kingdom and his righteousness,
and all these things will be given to you as well.*

Matthew 6:33

Prioritizing your relationship with Jesus means putting things in the right order. Spending time seeking Jesus and His kingdom helps produce more happiness, peace, perseverance, endurance, confidence, and overall Christlikeness in your life. Seeking Jesus is the antidote to anxiety, fear, and melancholy.

We live in a difficult world, and every day brings new pressures and scenarios. All are reasons we need Jesus. Placing Jesus and His way first in our lives creates the balance we desperately need. When there is fear, Jesus's presence and truth helps bring light to that darkness. When there is uncertainty, connecting to Jesus helps us find answers and a direction to take.

A life of seeking Jesus is a life well spent, as the Lord will fill your cup with unbelievable spiritual blessings that lead you to become more like Him and bring harmony, joy, and strength to your everyday life. The more you intentionally seek Jesus, the more fulfilled you will become.

▶ Reflection
Journal about your hopes and desires for your time with Jesus throughout this devotional.

DO YOU REALIZE WHO HE IS?

He said to his disciples, "Why are you so afraid?
Do you still have no faith?" They were terrified and
asked each other, "Who is this? Even the wind and
the waves obey him!"

Mark 4:40-41

Jesus's three-year ministry trek can be viewed as a
powerful and mighty proclamation of who He really is.
The miracles, the healings, the teachings show Jesus's
authority over all things. But even the disciples, who were
closest to Jesus, saw much of this work and still couldn't
wrap their minds around who Christ was.

How much more difficult is it for us, who were not
witnesses to Jesus's earthly ministry?

That is why our time with Jesus, through study, reflection, and prayer, is so vital to our walk. It helps us see and
remember just who Jesus is so that we can walk boldly in
His guidance, strength, and love.

Understanding and growing in your relationship with
Jesus is what enables you to be like Him. It helps you
banish anxiety, fear, insecurity, and confusion.

▶ Reflection
Reflect on who Jesus is to you. What has He done in
your life that shows you who He is? What do you desire
to learn more from Him?

JESUS REVEALS HIMSELF TO US

They asked each other, "Were not our hearts burning within us while he talked with us on the road and opened the Scriptures to us?"

Luke 24:32

After the Resurrection, but before all the disciples knew Jesus was alive, a few of His followers encountered Him walking on the road. Although they did not immediately recognize Him, they had a common reaction that felt like a burning within their hearts.

Have you ever experienced this when you've come close to Jesus? Some people describe an experience like burning in their heart when God is at work in their lives or when He speaks to them. This may happen during worship, while hearing a sermon, or when another person tells us just what we need to hear at the right time.

When you live like Jesus, the burning in your heart intensifies because you purposefully encounter God more often. Setting aside time to spend with Jesus will open your perception that God is always with you, and you will be able to discern and feel Him working in your life more frequently.

▶ Prayer
Lord, I want to have my heart burn for You and sense Your presence more in my life. Help me grow closer to You. Amen.

WE ARE CALLED TO BE HUMBLE

For even the Son of Man did not come to be served, but to serve, and to give his life as a ransom for many.

Mark 10:45

It would have been completely understandable, even expected, if Jesus had been worshipped when He came into this world. As God, He should have experienced so much recognition and praise here on Earth, but He never sought that. Instead, the opposite was true. Although Jesus did draw large crowds for a brief period in His ministry, it was never for the sake of receiving praise but as a sign to humanity that God's plan of redemption was coming to fruition.

Jesus lowered Himself, becoming human to show others how God wants us to live in humility. If Jesus, who was fully God and fully human, could do that, we can try to follow in His footsteps.

Jesus lived unlike anyone else. He gave Himself completely to the will of the Father, which led to His lifestyle of humility. God calls all of us to walk in the steps of Jesus, staying humble and obeying His will.

▸ Reflection

Imagine for a minute that you are Jesus, God on Earth, and you're unable to receive any recognition or praise. Instead, you live in complete humility, serving others. What would that be like?

JESUS KNEW
WHERE TO BE

*Why were you searching for me? Didn't you know
I had to be in my Father's house?*

Luke 2:49

This peek into Jesus's childhood offers us a rare and treasured insight. Although there is virtually nothing in scripture about Jesus during His teen or young adult years, we do have this one story about twelve-year-old Jesus wandering from Mary and Joseph to spend time in the Temple, His Father's house.

We see so much about Jesus's heart in this early story, where He is drawn to be close to His Father, God. That thirst Jesus has for intimacy with the Father clues us in to how to live like Jesus. It is so foundational that even as a child, Jesus longed for closeness with His Father. Whether we realize it or not, we, too, long for closeness with the Lord, and the more time we spend dwelling in His presence and reading His Word, the more fulfilled we will become. So be like twelve-year-old Jesus. When you find yourself longing to be close to the Father, spend some time in His house.

▶ Prayer

*God, I yearn for You as twelve-year-old Jesus did. Let
me search for Your presence and dwell in Your house
forever. Amen.*

JESUS'S WORDS ARE TIMELESS

Heaven and earth will pass away, but my words will never pass away.

Luke 21:33

The words of Jesus still impact humanity two thousand years later. That's because His words are exactly what every human heart needs to hear and understand. Jesus came to help us find our way back to God, and He left His timeless wisdom for us to refer to, to know how to live His way. We can find our way through every situation in life by leaning on Jesus's words.

His words are powerful and rejuvenating. They are markers on the often-murky path of life's difficulties. Decisions we need to make or demands placed on us can be overwhelming, but Jesus's words can penetrate any situation and bring light to show us the way.

Living like Jesus means taking hold of His teachings and folding His words and truth into our daily life in all circumstances—in our worries, fears, and anxieties. Jesus's words were meant to reach us here and now, two thousand years later, with their everlasting life and power.

▸ Reflection

Recall some of your favorite words of Jesus. What are they and what do they mean to you?

BELIEF IS
THE FIRST STEP

*[The man said,] "But if you can do anything, take
pity on us and help us." "'If you can'?" said Jesus.
"Everything is possible for one who believes."*

Mark 9:22-23

Anything is possible through Jesus. Even death couldn't
hold Him back. Jesus is unstoppable. In today's scripture, Jesus assures that it is our belief in Him that brings
hope and healing because Jesus can bring healing to any
situation. However, it is important to remember that our
belief does not mean God will always answer in the way
we expect.

Belief is a primary step for a follower of Jesus. It is what
we need in order to begin the discipleship process. If you
have been a Christian for any amount of time, there has
probably been a point where your belief in Jesus brought
you to healing or a new depth in your relationship
with Him.

Over time, our belief in Jesus can dull and fade,
especially if we have faced trials, hardships, or disappoint-
ments. We can forget what Jesus is capable of. But we can
find strength and direction by remembering who He is
and what He can do in our circumstances, and return to
our belief in His ability to directly impact our lives.

▶ Reflection

*How did you come to know Jesus? What drew you to
believe and follow Him? Spend a few minutes reflecting
on your faith journey by writing in your journal.*

FAITH MAKES
THINGS HAPPEN

Truly I tell you, if you have faith as small as a mustard seed, you can say to this mountain, "Move from here to there," and it will move. Nothing will be impossible for you.

Matthew 17:20

Jesus explains in this verse that faith in Him is the key to doing mighty, powerful, and astonishing things. As stated in the previous devotion, belief in Jesus is the first step. But to live like Him, Jesus calls us to a whole lifestyle of faith, leaning on Him in all situations, large and small. According to Jesus, even the smallest amount of faith will lead to mighty things.

Faith means trusting Jesus beyond our current plight or understanding, entrusting our fears and anxieties to Him, and believing that He is working for our good behind the scenes even if we can't see the mountain moving. Faith like this makes all things possible, even in seemingly impossible scenarios.

As we spend time with Jesus, our belief will transform into a resilient faith that makes powerful things happen.

▶ Reflection

Evaluate your faith in Jesus. Has there been a time in your life when your faith carried you during a difficult time?

JESUS ISN'T IN A HURRY WITH YOU

*At daybreak, Jesus went out to a solitary place.
The people were looking for him and when they
came to where he was, they tried to keep him from
leaving them.*

Luke 4:42

Could you imagine if Jesus came to your neighborhood to teach and performed all kinds of healings and miracles? You probably wouldn't want Him to leave, either, like the people in today's passage. This is the difference between Jesus's ministry then and how He operates today. Jesus never leaves your side now. He is not hurrying you.

Because Jesus was on a very specific mission in His earthly ministry, He couldn't dwell too long in one place. He needed to be as expansive as possible. He was always on the go. But although that was true for His earthly ministry, it isn't true for His work here and now. Jesus isn't eager to go tend to someone else. He simply wants to spend time with you. Everything you long for from Jesus is available and ready for you as you meet with Him and grow closer to Him. He won't ever move on from you.

▸ Prayer
Jesus, thank You for always being available for me and in no rush to leave my side. Thank You for staying with me for as long as I need You. Amen.

SUBMIT TO THE WILL OF GOD

Whoever does not take up their cross and follow me is not worthy of me. Whoever finds their life will lose it, and whoever loses their life for my sake will find it.

Matthew 10:38-39

One of my seminary professors would often say, "Our calling is to die." Rough calling, right? He meant that we are called to follow Jesus to all the places He went, including the cross. Although we will likely not be crucified for following Jesus, it helps if we keep in mind that Jesus is speaking metaphorically to us in the words from today's passage. To be like Jesus means being willing to go wherever God calls.

Jesus led a life of submission to God's will. Living like Jesus is following in the footsteps that Christ molded. Taking up our cross means sometimes doing the things we may not want to do but that God asks us to do, and in this stance, God will lead us to beautiful and redemptive things, just like the cross led to an empty grave. In this submission to the will of God, we find ourselves living like Jesus and finding unbelievable blessings and outcomes.

▶ Reflection
Think about something scary or uncomfortable God may be calling you to do, and journal about your willingness (or unwillingness) to do it.

JESUS SETS US FREE

Do not think that I have come to abolish the Law or the Prophets; I have not come to abolish them but to fulfill them.

Matthew 5:17

Sometimes it can feel as though there is a checklist of things that will keep God happy with us. Before Jesus there was the Law, the Old Testament rules the Israelites needed to follow. When Jesus arrived, He didn't come to abolish the Law but to fulfill it in such a way that we now only need faith in Him.

For a long time, God used the Law as a way to keep His people close to Him. But because Jesus made the way to God possible through His sacrifice, we no longer have to fulfill the Law to please God. Instead, we are free through Jesus.

Understanding this is vital to our relationship with Jesus. God seeks *us*, not rituals or formalities. He wants a relationship with our heart first. Then God's commands will no longer feel like a burden but something we do out of love for Him, which leads to immense freedom in our lives.

▸ Prayer

Jesus, thank You for judging me by my heart and not by how many "good deed" boxes I check off. Help me live in the freedom You offer as this brings peace to my life. Amen.

YOU DON'T NEED TO WORK SO HARD

Simon answered, "Master, we've worked hard all night and haven't caught anything. But because you say so, I will let down the nets."

Luke 5:5

Have you ever worked hard but seen few results? Are you exhausted from efforts that are still coming up short? Simon Peter experienced that hardship, too. In this scripture, he has spent all night on the boat, working diligently to produce a good catch, but there are no fish in his nets. Peter depended on fish for income, and the stress of his failure was no doubt trying for him. Whether you're dealing with financial issues or unrealized dreams, you, too, have probably cast your net out in the water only to find it empty.

Jesus overflowed Peter's net with fish. He gave Peter more than he could ever have expected because Peter trusted in what Jesus told Him, even while still struggling to believe.

Jesus offers you the same thing. If you have tried everything in your power to produce something in your life, maybe the answer is to lay down your way of doing things and entrust your direction to Jesus.

▶ Reflection
When things are not working out for you, do you find yourself trying harder, giving up, or asking Jesus for help?

JESUS WAS UNSHAKEABLE

He began by saying to them, "Today this scripture is fulfilled in your hearing."

Luke 4:21

Early on in Jesus's ministry, He revealed He was the Son of God. Jesus wasn't afraid of how scandalous that sounded to the people in the Temple. He knew who He was. The people of Israel had longed for centuries for the Messiah to come, but when He came, not everyone liked Him or His message. However, that didn't change the way Jesus pursued His mission. He was unshakeable in faith and truth.

Living like Jesus means finding your identity, strength, and security in Him, no matter who questions you, criticizes your faith, or tries to make you feel inferior. Sometimes that can feel overwhelming, especially when people try to discredit you, or feelings of insecurity arise. To live like Jesus means clinging to Him and His way as the source of your strength and identity. The more you root yourself in Jesus, the more unshakeable you will become.

▶ Reflection

Journal on how you feel about yourself as a Christian and where your strength comes from. What would it be like to gain more of Jesus's strength in your life?

BE READY FOR OPPORTUNITIES

Jesus went throughout Galilee, teaching in their synagogues, proclaiming the good news of the kingdom, and healing every disease and sickness among the people.

Matthew 4:23

The goal of Jesus's ministry might be summed up in this verse from Matthew. For three years, Jesus took every opportunity to bring glory to His Father by teaching, healing, and proclaiming the good news to the world. As He preached, He drew crowds and performed mighty, life-changing miracles for many.

Jesus lived a life of teaching and healing. We can follow in these footsteps by testifying to God's work in our lives and responding to those around us who are hurting. Although we may not all have the spiritual gift to teach or preach, we can all be ready for God's prompting. Jesus took the opportunities placed before Him to showcase God's power, love, and truth. When we stay close to Jesus, He grows in us the capability to respond to any opportunities God sends our way.

▶ Prayer

Lord, help me be willing and ready to go when opportunities arise to do Your work and share Your goodness and love with others. Let my life be like Yours, Jesus. Amen.

DON'T WORRY ABOUT TOMORROW

Therefore do not worry about tomorrow, for tomorrow will worry about itself. Each day has enough trouble of its own.

Matthew 6:34

Living like Jesus means entrusting our worries to Him.

It is ridiculously easy to get caught up in all our adult responsibilities. There are a lot of pressures and expectations placed on us. Being proactive and diligent in our work and life's demands is a very good thing, but we shouldn't be overwhelmingly burdened with responsibilities. Jesus calls us to be present in this day and not stress about tomorrow's problems.

Jesus is already preparing the way forward for tomorrow. He simply wants you to rest in His presence and to gather your strength in Him for whatever each day brings. Entrust the future to Jesus and grab hold of His hand today. He already understands the needs in front of you.

Whenever pressure or tension rises in your life, remember God is with you always and will see you through anything. Whether it comes in the form of inner strength, a more manageable schedule, a friend to talk to, or guidance from a professional, ask the Lord to help alleviate your worry by providing you with what you need.

▶ Activity

Make it a goal to write down every future problem on a sheet of paper and then add, "This is for Jesus to lead me through."

16

JESUS SEES
HIDDEN POTENTIAL

[Simon Peter and Andrew] were casting a net into the lake, for they were fishermen. "Come, follow me," Jesus said, "and I will send you out to fish for people."

Matthew 4:18-19

Jesus was attentive in His earthly ministry. Early on, Jesus looked for disciples, people He could mentor and teach. Jesus saw potential in places where others did not. For instance, when Jesus saw two common fishermen working rigorously on the water, He called out to them, offering a new life, a future, a place in His tribe.

Jesus saw more than what met the eye. He viewed status differently. That's what makes Jesus so welcoming. No matter who we are, we can have a place in Jesus's movement.

We can live like Jesus by being open to people, by seeing beyond their flaws, their status, or the way society sees them. We can live a life like Jesus by asking God to help us value the heart and the potential in people.

▶ Prayer

Jesus, help me see hidden potential in all people, regardless of their status in life. I want to see what You see in others. Amen.

BE BOLD
IN YOUR PRAYERS

*Father, if you are willing, take this cup from me; yet
not my will, but yours be done.*

Luke 22:42

Nothing was off-limits in Jesus's prayer to the Father.

Just before His arrest and death, Jesus prepared
Himself for His trial by praying in the Garden of
Gethsemane. Jesus understood His mission was to die,
yet in this scripture we still see Him asking God to take
this objective off His plate. Jesus appealed to His Father
with the trust of a child, and just as a child of a loving
parent is authentic and bold in their requests, so was
Jesus when He prayed in the garden.

Throughout His ministry, Jesus taught us to approach
God like little children because God is our Father, too. He
demonstrates what this looks like in this prayer from His
final night on earth.

There is nothing off-limits in our prayers to God. Jesus
modeled for us that it is safe and good to be honest and
transparent in our prayers to the Lord. We are privileged
to be able to come to such a loving and understanding
Father when we pray, just like Jesus did.

▶ Activity
*Spend some time praying to the Father authentically
and boldly about whatever is weighing you down today.*

JESUS IS OUR
ONLY OBLIGATION

But Jesus told him, "Follow me, and let the dead bury their own dead."

Matthew 8:22

Living like Jesus isn't always easy. God calls us to put everything else aside and follow Him whenever He calls. In today's scripture, Jesus speaks to someone who does want to follow Jesus but has an important obligation to take care of first.

The lesson in this exchange is that there will always be distractions, obligations, and responsibilities that can take our attention from Jesus and place it on other situations we face. Jesus is trying to teach us to put Him first, before everything else.

By placing Jesus first, we practice the proper order of our lives. Once we do that, we will be able to receive Jesus's stability and direction, which will enable us to fulfill our obligations through His strength. But when we let life's situations come before Jesus, we lose our focus and, often, our strength.

▸ Reflection

Reflect on your own responses to your obligations. Do you find yourself dwelling in the Lord's presence and seeking His guidance? Why or why not?

THE VALUE OF
GOD'S KINGDOM

*Again, the kingdom of heaven is like a merchant
looking for fine pearls. When he found one of great
value, he went away and sold everything he had
and bought it.*

Matthew 13:45-46

In this short parable, Jesus explains that the Gospel—
living like Jesus—is very much like finding a very valuable
pearl. Although the merchant in the parable can't afford
the pearl, he understands its worth and sells everything in
order to acquire this rarity.

Jesus calls us to this same kind of life. Jesus likens
God's kingdom to a rare and highly valuable treasure that
is worth liquidating all our assets to purchase.

Often, we act as though status symbols, money, and
other people's opinions are of greater importance than
seeking after God, but Jesus knew that kingdom living
far outweighed the wavering accolades of others and
the perishing goods of this world. Following God's commands has eternal rewards and pays dividends such as
peace, joy, and perseverance that supersede any earthly
treasures.

▶ Reflection
*Think about your most prized possession and contrast
its value with how you think about your relationship
with God. How do they compare?*

THE THINGS
THAT IMPRESSED JESUS

*They all gave out of their wealth; but she, out
of her poverty, put in everything—all she had to
live on.*

Mark 12:44

What impressed Jesus the most was the true motivations
of people. While in the Temple observing the rituals, Jesus
noted that the rich people gave some of their money,
whereas one widow came in with practically nothing to
her name and gave what would have seemed insignifi-
cant to most but was a large amount for her.

Jesus knew that the widow gave proportionately more
than the rich because she gave almost all that she had. He
calls us, His disciples, to give as much as we can, even if it
challenges and stretches us.

Living like Jesus means taking hold of His teachings
and shaping your life around them. Jesus rewards the
person whose generosity comes from a place of authenticity and gratitude, without obligation. So much of
Jesus's ministry was about confronting people's motivations and searching for authenticity in their outward
expressions of faith. Remember, what impresses people
isn't always what impresses God.

▶ Reflection

*Take note of things people do that impress you. Are
they the same things Jesus would value? Why or
why not?*

JESUS'S PASSIONATE JUSTICE

When Jesus entered the temple courts, he began to drive out those who were selling. "It is written," he said to them, "'My house will be a house of prayer'; but you have made it 'a den of robbers.'"

Luke 19:45-46

Nowhere else in scripture do we find Jesus acting seemingly so out of character, full of anger as He drives the merchants from the Temple. Jesus's unusual behavior is a clue to the situation's importance. Throughout all the questioning and challenging of His identity and authority, Jesus didn't usually respond to His naysayers with outbursts. However, the Temple was the representation of God's presence on Earth, and Jesus wanted to protect its sacredness.

Jesus saw God's house become a marketplace, making a spectacle of God's Word and Law. This is a rare glimpse into Jesus's passionate justice, which was often held at bay throughout His ministry.

Although we are called to be loving and compassionate, we are also called to standards. It's often easier to not say anything when people behave poorly, but that isn't what Jesus modeled. He stood up for injustice when it was called for, and we should likewise be inspired to stand up for our beliefs in this world.

▶ Prayer
Jesus, help me be confident and strong when standing up for injustice like You did. Amen.

NOTHING INTIMIDATED JESUS

All the people were amazed and said to each other, "What words these are! With authority and power he gives orders to impure spirits and they come out!"

Luke 4:36

Jesus spoke with such authority and power that nothing, not even evil, could stand in His way. Jesus was fearless because He knew who He was and He knew His purpose. We can get tripped up from time to time because we forget who we are and who Jesus is. Even an unkind word or a disappointment can rattle or devastate us. In times like these, we rally by fixing our eyes on Jesus and living like He did. He stood fearless and spoke powerful truths to rectify situations, which can be intimidating for us to do. But the truth is freeing. We can be like Jesus by rooting ourselves in God's presence wherever we go. When we know God is always at our side, it solidifies us and helps alleviate feelings of intimidation and fear.

It's a given that life throws a lot of curveballs, but what is stable and true is the Lord's presence with us always. Lean into His presence and it will build deep faith and fortitude in you to withstand even the hardest trials.

▶ Activity
Spend time listing things that help raise your confidence and enable you to stand stronger in Jesus. Write down five Bible verses that describe who Jesus is and that can help you gain strength in the Lord.

JESUS IS THE WAY TO PERFECTION

Then he said to them, "The Sabbath was made for man, not man for the Sabbath. So the Son of Man is Lord even of the Sabbath."

Mark 2:27–28

In Jesus's time, people drew close to God through observance of the Law. They would follow the mandated rules to strive to be perfect in God's sight. Religious leaders were obsessed with staying in God's good graces, so they became rigid and vigilant in making sure God's people were following the Law. But even with all those rules, God's presence didn't dwell in them the way the Holy Spirit resides within you right now.

Jesus knew the Law would no longer be the only way to God because faith in Him would replace the rules, like the one in today's scripture: that no labor could be done on the Sabbath.

As followers of Jesus, we can get caught up in trying to be perfect, too. We may think coming close to Jesus means following all the rules and never making a mistake. But Jesus came because we do make mistakes, and He paves the way forward. Jesus doesn't want you to be perfect. He wants you to trust in His perfection and mercy as the way to be reconciled to God.

▶ Prayer

Jesus, thank You for Your mercy when I make mistakes. It is through Your perfection, not mine, that I am made perfect. Amen.

BE DESPERATE
FOR JESUS

"Your daughter is dead," they said. "Why bother the teacher anymore?" Overhearing what they said, Jesus told him, "Don't be afraid; just believe."

Mark 5:35–36

We can sometimes feel as though we are a nuisance, a bother to Jesus. Nothing could be further from the truth. Jesus's function is to be our light, our truth, and our way. Jesus is here to help us.

In today's scripture we see that Jesus isn't bothered when the synagogue leader, Jairus, interrupts His teaching. In fact, Jesus is impressed that Jairus is so bold and filled with faith as to desperately seek Him in this way.

No matter how big or small our problems are, Jesus calls us to act like Jairus and run to Him for the answers. Jairus's daughter has died, and his situation seems impossible. But he has heard about Jesus's ability to do mighty and powerful things, so he seeks Jesus out of his tremendous faith.

This is who Jesus is. He is our healer and companion, and He responds to those who are desperate for Him. Jesus is never bothered by us.

▶ Activity

Imagine you are Jairus, standing in front of Jesus, looking for help in an impossible situation. What does Jesus say to you? How does that translate to your life today?

JESUS IS
CONCERNED WITH
HEART CONDITIONS

Nothing outside a person can defile them by going into them. Rather, it is what comes out of a person that defiles them.

Mark 7:15

Faith can be reduced to rituals—go to church, take communion, pray the same prayers—so much so that it is easy to make it look like you are doing great in your belief. But Jesus was never fooled by appearances. He always cut straight to the heart, the inner workings of a person. We can dress up, but we may still have a misguided heart or behaviors that are not in line with the gospel. Then the core of who we are comes out, not in our outward appearance but in our words and actions.

People in Jesus's time were constantly concerned with being in line with God's Law because its customs made them feel safe and secure with God. But Jesus came to pave a new path to security with God that focused not as much on rituals but on the condition of the heart.

Prayers and church services are wonderful ways to worship. But Jesus doesn't want us to seek stability only in appearances or customs. He wants us all to be pure from the inside out.

▸ Prayer

Jesus, make me whole from the inside out. Help me move beyond seeking Your approval in empty practices. Grow and transform my inner self. Amen.

DOING THE RIGHT THING CAN COME WITH A COST

Everyone will hate you because of me. But not a hair of your head will perish. Stand firm, and you will win life.

Luke 21:17–19

Have you ever had an experience where you did the right thing but it ended up hurting you? We often see this in childhood, where a child is being bullied and another kid steps in to stand up for the victim, only to find themselves another target for the bully. We will unfortunately find throughout our lives that doing the right thing sometimes comes with a cost.

Jesus taught this principle to the disciples as He prepared them for life after Him. As the disciples became messengers of the good news, they themselves became targeted, as Jesus had been. Following Jesus doesn't come without hardship, even though it is incredibly rewarding. Jesus offers a countercultural message and way of life that naturally creates tension. If you ever find yourself doing something that is in line with Jesus, and you get a hardship as a result, remember that Jesus lived this life daily and sympathizes with your plight.

▶ Reflection

Have you ever done something good or in the name of God that didn't go the way you hoped? Journal about that experience and take your feelings to the Lord in prayer.

TURN THE OTHER CHEEK

But I tell you, do not resist an evil person. If anyone slaps you on the right cheek, turn to them the other cheek also.

Matthew 5:39

Turning the other cheek doesn't mean we should stay in toxic relationships or harmful situations. God loves us and wants us to seek help and safety when it's needed. What Jesus is asking is for us not to pursue battles, seek revenge, or repay insult with insult. Instead, He wants us to turn our hurts over to Him and let Him handle it.

It's hard not to retaliate when someone has hurt you. But to live like Jesus is to follow His wisdom and commands, even when they feel counterintuitive or difficult. Jesus never asks His followers to do impossible things, however. Instead, when we ask for help, He equips us through His power, strength, and love, guiding us through the process in His way and on His timetable.

▶ Reflection

Journal about how this command from Jesus makes you feel and what your personal experience with turning the other cheek has been.

GIVE FREELY

Give to the one who asks you, and do not turn away from the one who wants to borrow from you.

Matthew 5:42

Jesus didn't own much in His lifetime and he lived without a home for years, so what He says in today's verse should make us pay attention. Generosity breeds good things in life. Have you ever seen a happy hoarder or a joyous miser? Typically, no, but you often find an effervescent giver!

Generosity is one of the foundations of living like Jesus. When possessions, time, or money become difficult to let go of, it stops us living a life like Jesus. We also lose the inner blessings that giving produces.

For many of us, gift-giving is our love language. Maybe it's yours, too; maybe giving someone the perfect gift is an honor that fills you with joy. When we make a gift for someone or give to them out of our time or resources, we are blessed, too. The more we can give freely, the more God can bless us with joy.

▶ Activity
Plan to do something unexpected for someone who needs lifting up. Possible ideas include dropping off a meal, giving a present, or helping with a task.

JESUS CALLS US TO LOOK AT OURSELVES

Why do you look at the speck of sawdust in your brother's eye and pay no attention to the plank in your own eye?

Matthew 7:3

It's ridiculously easy to see other people's problems. It's almost an art form we humans have created, identifying what might be wrong with someone else. Yet, we rarely check our own behavior or patterns to see where we may be struggling. It's hard to see our own problems, isn't it?

We tend to examine another's issues while neglecting our own. To live like Jesus, let's look to His cutting wisdom in today's scripture.

Jesus always knew what was at the heart of humanity; it's why He came in the first place. His teaching about focusing on oneself instead of other people is invaluable. When we focus on others, we sit in a seat of judgment that should be reserved only for God. Each of us is no better than anyone else, and we all need a Savior. By focusing on the faults of others, we are virtually equating ourselves to God and His ability to judge.

▸ Prayer
Lord, help me get rid of the desire to judge the failings of others and focus only on my issues. Amen.

SHINE JESUS'S LIGHT

In the same way, let your light shine before others, that they may see your good deeds and glorify your Father in heaven.

Matthew 5:16

One of my favorite things about Jesus and the Gospels is that Jesus invites us to partake in the kingdom, to be beacons of light in the world. As we shine Jesus's light toward others, God fills our hearts with exuberant joy and we become part of something bigger.

The world around us is hurting. People are suffering and need Jesus to be shown to them. You have an open invitation to be part of the solution through simple acts of kindness done out of love for Jesus. These can be little things, such as opening doors for others, smiling at strangers, or looking for opportunities to compliment people. The world desperately needs more kindness and love in it, so be like Jesus and shine His light everywhere you go.

▸ Activity

Choose five random acts of kindness to spread Jesus's light into the world this week.

JESUS BRINGS
US PEACE

Peace I leave with you; my peace I give you. I do not give to you as the world gives. Do not let your hearts be troubled and do not be afraid.

John 14:27

Living like Jesus produces peace in your life. It is one of the most amazing and fulfilling gifts Jesus brings to His followers. Peace can be elusive in our anxious, tense world, but it is the antidote to the disharmony that worry and fear bring.

The closer you stay to Jesus and abide in His truth, the more God will bless you with His peace and the other fruits of the Spirit. As Jesus says in today's scripture, the peace He gives is different from the world's peace. Often, we can feel peace for a fleeting moment after we overcome an issue, but God's peace comes from a never-ending source. You will never run dry of His peace, so long as you keep your eyes on Him. He will fill you up until your cup overflows.

▶ Reflection

Journal your thoughts about peace. What has your experience been with peace in your own life? How might Jesus's peace enhance your life?

MODEL GENEROSITY LIKE JESUS

But when you give to the needy, do not let your left hand know what your right hand is doing, so that your giving may be in secret.

Matthew 6:3-4

Being generous is important to God because God is generous to us. God always expects His followers to embody the same things He offers. To live like Jesus is to do good deeds in secret, not to try to earn attention and praise from our benevolent acts. Jesus wants us to give in secret so we don't stoke the flame of pride that can come from giving. To truly be generous and live to serve others means that giving is done solely for the recipient, not for personal gain.

Jesus lived His life by sacrificing everything, including His own life, so that we could be saved. In the same way, we are called to give selflessly to those in need because we love God and love them and want to embody the life of Jesus in our acts.

▶ Prayer
Lord, reveal to me the motivations behind my giving and help me model Jesus when helping those less fortunate. Amen.

GOD IS
IN CONTROL

Your kingdom come, your will be done, on earth as it is in heaven. Give us today our daily bread.

Matthew 6:10-11

Today's scripture is a portion of the Lord's Prayer. When the disciples asked Jesus how they should pray, Jesus responded with what we call the Lord's Prayer, or the "Our Father." Its purpose was to help the disciples—and us—understand that everything we need in life, from help with our troubles to daily provisions, comes from the Lord.

Jesus taught this prayer to help His followers understand that God truly is in control, He even provides the daily bread of our meals, provisions, and spiritual "food." God knows what's best and just what we need.

The more we rely on Him and turn to Him in prayer, the more we will see the work of His provision in our lives. In the Lord's Prayer, Jesus gave us a beautifully concise prayer for everyday life. It's simple, and it places our focus on God, who sustains life and is truly in control and provides for our every need.

▶ Activity
Pray the Lord's prayer each day this week and ask God to increase your faith in His provisions and direction in your life.

STANDING FIRM
IN TRUTH

Jesus answered, "It is said: 'Do not put the Lord your God to the test.'"

Luke 4:12

One way we live like Jesus is to view God like He did. While being tempted by the devil in the desert, Jesus refuted him by standing in truth and communicating that truth. Jesus would not allow anyone to test Him. He lived in bold truth and was unwavering in His desire to honor God.

Jesus's truth wasn't dependent on how He felt. It wasn't relative. Rather, He lived God's timeless wisdom, which did not change with popular thought or current trends. Sometimes we can waver in truth or feel uneasy when confronted, but the more we allow God to be the center of who we are and follow His commands, the stronger and more like Jesus we become. God will enable you to stand firmly in truth no matter how scary the opponent may be, just as Jesus did in the wilderness.

▸ Prayer

Jesus, I want to be fearless and bold when opponents come my way. I want to stand in Your truth and be unwavering. Help me be like You. Amen.

THROW IT AWAY

And if your right hand causes you to stumble, cut it off and throw it away. It is better for you to lose one part of your body than for your whole body to go into hell.

Matthew 5:30

Jesus was very serious when it came to behaviors that led to problems or sin. In today's scripture, Jesus teaches about the dangers of not taking seriously the effects of sin. He likens sin to a malfunctioning body part, saying it would be better to remove the problematic part entirely. Jesus is speaking figuratively about the danger of sin and how infectious and cancerous it is to our souls.

Sometimes we struggle with sins that we can simply cut off. Sins such as gossiping, lying, or unfaithfulness to a partner are all behaviors we can stop if we choose to. Some sinful behaviors may take more time than others to eliminate, but the ball is always in our court. We live like Jesus when we treat sin as a disease in our lives and work on cutting it out; we can do this by drawing our strength from Jesus.

▶ Reflection

Is there a sin you are struggling with? Journal about why the sin is hard to let go of and how God can help you cut it out of your life.

WHO DO YOU LISTEN TO?

Watch out for false prophets. They come to you in sheep's clothing, but inwardly they are ferocious wolves. By their fruit you will recognize them.

Matthew 7:15–16

Jesus understood there would be a lot of people representing Him and His message, but not everyone who proclaims God has holy motives. False prophets, as Jesus described them, are people who sound and even look like people of God, claiming to speak on His behalf, but who aren't necessarily living in line with His teachings and can lead you down the wrong path.

Sometimes, people without your best interests at heart can influence you without you being aware of it. That is why it is important to always bring people's biblical teachings or proclamations about God to the Lord. At any time, you can ask God if a message or directive is from Him. He will illuminate the situation and help you discern whether this is a person you should follow.

Just because someone says they are a person of God doesn't always mean they truly represent God. As Jesus said, you will recognize them by their fruit: a life that resembles Christ's sacrificial and humble life. We live like Jesus when we seek God's help in discerning who to listen to and follow.

▶ Prayer
Lord, help me develop wisdom and discernment. Let me follow only Your way and Your truth. Amen.

BUILDING YOUR LIFE ON JESUS'S TEACHINGS

Therefore everyone who hears these words of mine and puts them into practice is like a wise man who built his house on the rock.

Matthew 7:24

At the end of Jesus's great teaching known as the Sermon on the Mount, He concludes with profound wisdom about putting His teachings into practice. Jesus says that listening to what He says is important, but He also wants us to apply it in our lives, to build our lives upon His teachings.

Jesus wasn't just a great teacher or prophet. He was the Son of God who came to show people how to be in a relationship with God. He came to bridge the gap between us and God through His teachings, death, and Resurrection.

Sure, we may like Jesus and His teachings, but it's often challenging to follow what He says, to allow His teachings to inform our decision making and transform our lives. Building our life on a solid rock of faith is to apply Jesus's teachings to our everyday life. This is how we live like Jesus.

▸ Prayer
Jesus, I want to apply Your teachings to my life so that my decision making is informed by Your teachings and my life is transformed into Your likeness. Amen.

JESUS'S
TEACHINGS ARE HARD

On hearing it, many of his disciples said, "This is a hard teaching. Who can accept it?" . . . From this time many of his disciples turned back and no longer followed him.

John 6:60, 66

Today's verse is a bit of a heartbreaking moment in Jesus's ministry life, when some people decided to stop following Him because His teachings were simply too difficult to adhere to. I've had many instances on my journey with Jesus when it felt too difficult to follow where He was leading. Fear, and stubbornness held me prisoner, keeping me stuck in my ways.

Although some of Jesus's teachings may seem impossible, He will guide us through. Jesus simply calls us to be open to His ways, His teaching, and His transformation.

When we are rigid and unwilling to follow where Jesus leads, He cannot really mold us and bring us to new levels of living like Him.

When I finally surrendered to what God was asking of me, Jesus grew me in ways I never dreamed. Although His teachings may be difficult at times, He is good and will see you through to the other side. Trust Him.

▶ Activity
Choose one thing Jesus may be calling you to do and take one step toward doing it so that you can grow more like Christ.

PART 2

▶ LOVE LIKE JESUS

Based on Jesus's teachings, this section offers a mixture of the love Jesus offers us and the love to which He calls us. I'm a firm believer that our love must stem from Jesus first before we can love like He does. Jesus wants to fill each of us with His love, and we need to keep returning to Him and abiding in Him as the source of the love we extend to others. Once we experience Jesus's love and grow in it, we are called to extend it to everyone we interact with. The devotions in this section will help you experience Jesus's love. They'll also present opportunities to fill up on His substantial, sustaining love so you can share it with others through your words and actions.

THE FIRST
COMMANDMENT IS
TO LOVE GOD

Jesus replied: "Love the Lord your God with all your heart and with all your soul and with all your mind.' This is the first and greatest commandment."

Matthew 22:37–38

Have you ever thought it strange or unusual that God commands us to love Him? Why are we commanded to love God?

You would think that we, as Christians, would find it easy to love God, that we wouldn't need to be told to do so. But if it was that easy and natural, we wouldn't need a command directing us. The truth is that it's so challenging, Jesus made it a point to tell us to love God above everything else. Why?

Well, it's because we have an enormous capacity to love ourselves over God. In fact, it's at the very core of our nature to seek our perceived needs and desires over placing God first. But it's not because God is vain or mean that He requires our love first and foremost; it's because it places us into the proper alignment of looking up to our Creator. Loving God helps keep us in check and our feet on solid ground.

▶ Reflection

Journal about your love for God. What does it mean to you? What has it done in your life? How has it informed your life?

LOVING OTHERS IS JUST AS IMPORTANT

And the second is like it: "Love your neighbor as yourself."

Matthew 22:39

In this verse, Jesus describes the second most essential commandment to our faith, which is to love our neighbor like we love ourselves. But who is our neighbor? In Jesus's estimation, any fellow human being is our neighbor because God created all of us and we all inhabit the same planet He provided for us. The Lord wants us to extend the love He continually gives us to those around us, strangers and friends alike. Everyone should receive the love God inspires us to give.

Of course, there are different kinds of love. The Lord isn't expecting you to love a stranger as closely as you love a family member. Boundaries are still important! But He is asking us to treat others with the kindness we long to receive ourselves. From our own families to strangers in a grocery store, we should look for opportunities to do loving acts of kindness and goodness to others, just like Jesus did.

▶ Activity

Challenge yourself this week to extend some form of love to every person you interact with, from sharing a loving smile to helping someone in a jam.

LOVE YOURSELF, TOO

He answered, "Love the Lord your God with all your heart and with all your soul and with all your strength and with all your mind"; and, "Love your neighbor as yourself."

Luke 10:27

One challenge of learning to love like Jesus is the conundrum of loving ourselves first. What if we simply don't love ourselves, or we don't do it in the way God intends? If our own self-love is broken, wouldn't that mean the love we extend to others is flawed, too?

This is why it is crucial to draw all our love and guidance from Jesus. He is the source of love. Through God's word and His presence in our lives, we grow in our knowledge of His love for us. When we feel loved by God, we find it easier to love ourselves and easier to love others. His perfect love overflows to those we interact with. Loving ourselves always stems from receiving love from God first. He is the gardener of love, the source of it all.

▶ Activity

What are your barriers regarding self-love? Spend some time loving yourself this week. Choose to do something you love that brings you joy and a self-esteem boost.

REMAIN IN JESUS'S LOVE

Jesus replied, "Anyone who loves me will obey my teaching. My Father will love them, and we will come to them and make our home with them."

John 14:23

The secret to loving like Jesus is staying connected to Jesus's love. Whether you feel it often or rarely, Jesus loves you immensely and is always extending His love and grace to you.

Simply put, the truth is that Jesus came to save you from your impending doom. He came to give you a relationship with Him and make your life full. That is love! He is with you always, and He will never leave you. Stay in that truth, no matter what feelings or doubts arise. Over time, Jesus's love will feel richer and more palpable to you so long as you remember the truth that His love never leaves you.

The more you cement that reality into the core of who you are, the more you will become like Jesus and enable His love to overtake your everyday life. Feelings are feelings, but truth is truth.

▶ Prayer

Jesus, thank You so much for Your love. I want Your love to inform every day so that it becomes the bedrock on which I build my life. Amen.

LOVE YOUR ENEMIES

But love your enemies, do good to them, and lend to them without expecting to get anything back. Then your reward will be great.

Luke 6:35

I don't know about you, but thinking about loving my enemies isn't something that warms my heart and fills it with joy. Quite the opposite. Confusion, anger, and feelings of injustice often come forth instead. Of course, that is when I've forgotten who God is and how He continually forgives me through Jesus's sacrifice.

We don't deserve grace. Jesus wasn't obligated to die on the cross for us. But He submitted to the will of His Father so Jesus's sacrifice could pay our debt and reconcile us to God. Loving our enemies can be achieved when we remember that Jesus loved them enough to sacrifice for them, too.

None of us deserve grace, yet Jesus extended it anyway. How can we not forgive others when Jesus broke His body to forgive us? Loving and forgiving others doesn't mean that it is safe to have a relationship with everyone, or to lower boundaries or allow harmful people into our lives, but forgiveness does loosen the chains within our hearts and frees us from within.

▶ Prayer
Jesus, I was once a sinner, but Your forgiveness and love saved me. Help me follow in Your footsteps and forgive my enemies as You forgave Yours.

THERE IS
A SOURCE FOR LOVE

As the Father has loved me, so have I loved you.
Now remain in my love.

John 15:9

Jesus's love came directly from God. This is a very important model for us. Because Jesus came to show us the way and demonstrate how to walk closely with God here on earth, everything He did is crucial for our relationship with God. Jesus modeled for us the reality that there is a formula for us to follow. He received love from His Father, and He took that inspiration and loved others because of it. God's love was His wellspring, the source that never dried up. That is what enabled Jesus to love so much: He stayed close to His Father and let God be the source of His love.

We can follow in the love of Jesus by following the same formula. If we receive our love from Jesus, as the disciples did, we can take that love and unleash it onto those in our world. This is how we love like Jesus.

▸ Prayer
Jesus, I want all my love to stem from You. Fill me up until my cup overflows with Your love. Amen.

BE MERCIFUL

Be merciful, just as your Father is merciful.

Luke 6:36

To show mercy is to provide kindness and forgiveness to someone who has done wrong and, we may often think, deserves punishment. As children of God, we confess that we have sinned, and we can all ask for God's forgiveness instead of punishment. This is the basis of Christianity. It is what Jesus came and claimed for us: eternal life and forgiveness from God.

Because we have all received forgiveness from God, He asks us to extend that same forgiveness to those who have wronged us, who have hurt us, who are our enemies. The Christian walk—living like Jesus—is not easy. It is hard because it goes against our self-protective instincts. God asks us to trust in His way, to lean on Him to forgive and extend mercy to others. God will enable you to be merciful, even to those it may seem impossible to forgive. Remember God's mercy for you and ask Him to change your heart.

▸ Journal

Recall some moments in your life where God or someone else showed you mercy. How did you feel? What did mercy enable you to do?

JESUS'S LOVE
WAS SACRIFICIAL

My command is this: Love each other as I have
loved you. Greater love has no one than this: to lay
down one's life for one's friends.

John 15:12-13

To love like Jesus means to love sacrificially, in line with
God's will. Sometimes when we hear the word "sacrificial"
we think of pain, but Jesus's sacrificial love didn't always
mean pain; there was only one cross and one death.
Furthermore, His death led to Resurrection, for Him then
and for us now.

Jesus placed high importance on the needs of the
others He served. His teachings were for the benefit of
others, not to prop Him up with power and influence. He
fed the hungry, knowing many would never follow Him
again after they were full. These are examples of sacrificial
love, of doing something with no intention of receiving
anything in return.

Jesus's whole life was an example of sacrificial love.
From His ministry life to His death to His actions after the
Resurrection, He came to serve others. In this, He pro-
vided us with an amazing example of pure love.

▶ Reflection
Reflect on your thoughts and feelings about sacrifice
and the concept of sacrificial love as displayed through
the life of Jesus.

MIRRORED LOVE

If you love those who love you, what reward will you get? Are not even the tax collectors doing that?

Matthew 5:46

It's not very hard to love people who are kind and good to us. In fact, it is rather easy and intuitive to be good to those who are nice. When someone shows us kindness, especially when it's unexpected, our usual reaction is warmth and even joy. However, if someone is rude, mean, or cruel, the natural reaction is to mirror those emotions back.

In today's scripture, Jesus tries to show that our love is often simply a looking glass, a reflection of what we have been given. He calls us to reflect His love onto others, despite their actions or how they treat us.

To love like Jesus means that the extension of your love is unaffected by the actions of others. He modeled this without flaw in His life. But the only way to truly make this happen is by allowing Jesus to continually shape your heart to be gentler, kinder, more like His.

▶ Prayer

Jesus, I want to be like You and love like You. Help my heart resemble Yours so no matter what anyone says or does I can always be Your agent of love in this world. Amen.

FINDING GOD THROUGH LOVE

Blessed are the pure in heart, for they will see God.

Matthew 5:8

It can often feel as though God is far away from us, even undetectable. As the world continues to grind and the culture of busyness takes over, we can feel overwhelmed by simple tasks and daily responsibilities. Finding God's presence in our daily lives can feel like finding a needle in a haystack when things are hectic.

Jesus teaches us that those who have a heart like His will see God. The more you allow Jesus to take center stage in your life, the more you spend time with Him and choose His ways over others, the more transformation you will see. This helps you discern God's presence in your life and see Him working even when you couldn't before.

Loving like Jesus and having a heart like His opens a whole new reality to you. Love helps you see things differently. Most importantly, loving like Jesus enables you to grow closer to God.

▶ Reflection
Journal about the current state of your heart and how much you think it reflects Jesus's own heart.

LOVE JESUS OVER YOUR FAMILY

Anyone who loves their father or mother more than me is not worthy of me; anyone who loves their son or daughter more than me is not worthy of me.

Matthew 10:37

Can you believe that Jesus calls us to love Him more than our only family, our children, our parents? Jesus isn't being rude, mean, or narcissistic by calling us to love Him supremely. He simply knows that He is the source of our love, and in order to love others appropriately, our love must stem solely from Him. When we place anything over Jesus—yes, even love of our family—our devotion becomes out of order and we attach ourselves to the wrong things.

The world emphasizes loving family above all else, but Jesus knows that loving Him first enables us to love our family *better*. Our family love will be richer and fuller when Jesus is the source of that love.

Jesus will never fail us or leave us. He is the epitome of love. That's why He wants us to know our love must originate from His love, which is perfect and flawless.

▸ Prayer
Jesus, help me understand that You are the source of my love for everyone. Help me place You over everything so I can love more fully. Amen.

THE DISCIPLE JESUS LOVED

One of them, the disciple whom Jesus loved, was reclining next to him.

John 13:23

I used to think it was obnoxious that John referred to himself as "the disciple whom Jesus loved." To me, it just seemed a little arrogant. However, as time passed, I began to understand that John was right in the way he presented himself. You see, John knew something that many of us don't fully grasp. He understood that his identity was directly linked to Jesus's love. He believed in this so much that it altered how he spoke of himself. In a sense, he changed his name to reflect the magnitude of Jesus and His love in his life.

Can you imagine knowing Jesus's love in such a way that it changes the way you identify yourself? This is what Jesus's love can do for you: It can transform how you see yourself, enabling you to describe yourself from the perspective of the light and love of Jesus.

▶ Activity

Create a short list of phrases you might use to describe your relationship with God. For example, "My guide in life is the Lord," "My worth comes from God," or "I am known and loved by God."

YOUR LOVE
ILLUMINATES JESUS

*By this everyone will know that you are my
disciples, if you love one another.*

John 13:35

Love is the language of Christianity and the instrument
of Jesus. Love defines us and tethers us to the Lord. Jesus
calls us, His disciples, to display His love to others. When
we do, we bear witness to Jesus's love as our motivation.
Unfortunately, sometimes the outside world sees hypocrisy,
judgment, or even hatred as the defining characteristics
of Christians—and sometimes Christians can fall victim to
these behaviors instead of reflecting God's love. The world
doesn't always look at Christians as agents of love; sometimes it's the opposite.

Although we are not responsible for how people per-
ceive us, we are responsible for how we follow Jesus's
call to live a lifestyle of love. Jesus only wants us to be
known by His love. We can love like Jesus by following in
His footsteps and always defaulting to love. His life was
defined by love, and ours should be as well.

▸ Reflection
*Reflect on how your love illuminates Jesus's impact in
your life. How can you share His love more intentionally?*

FUELED BY LOVE

For God so loved the world that he gave his one and only Son, that whoever believes in him shall not perish but have eternal life.

John 3:16

From athletes wearing John 3:16 to street evangelists quoting it, this Bible verse is probably one of the most popular in all of scripture, perhaps because it's a very succinct presentation of the Gospel and describes God's redeeming plan in an easily digestible statement.

Jesus came to Earth because of love, and knowing Jesus's motivation is paramount to understanding how to be like Jesus and how to love like Jesus. You really cannot divorce love from Jesus; the two are interchangeable. Because Jesus is part of God, His mission from God was fueled by love.

Everything Jesus did was because of love and everything Jesus does for you is out of love. To love like Jesus, love must be the basis of all that you are and all that you do.

▸ Prayer

Jesus, I want to be fueled by love just like You are. I want everything I do to have a symphony of love wrapped around it. Amen.

SHOCKING LOVE

Jesus said, "Father forgive them, for they do not know what they are doing." And they divided up his clothes by casting lots.

Luke 23:34

Can you imagine what Jesus was going through when He uttered these words while dying, innocent, on the cross? After being arrested, mocked, judged, and beaten, Jesus looked into the crowd as the soldiers gambled over His garments, and He said a prayer for them. With His dying breath, Jesus turned to His Father out of compassion for the broken nature of humanity and prayed on their behalf as they mocked Him. It's hard to imagine having that grace in such a moment of brutal agony. But that is our Lord, that is Jesus—the agent of love—on full display, never faltering from His lifestyle of love.

Jesus never failed because there was no separation between Him and love. They were interconnected because He was, and is, love. Praying for those people wasn't emotionally difficult for Jesus to do. It's just who Jesus was.

▶ Reflection

Imagine it was you on the cross while people around you were mocking and hurting you. What would be your response, and how does that compare with Jesus's reaction?

SPEAKING TRUTH IN LOVE

*Jesus answered, "If you want to be perfect, go, sell
your possessions and give to the poor, and you
will have treasure in heaven. Then come, follow
me." When the young man heard this, he went
away sad, because he had great wealth.*

Matthew 19:21–22

Some people have a flawed understanding of Jesus that
leads them to equate His love and ministry with being
passive and even weak. But there was nothing weak about
Jesus. He was strong, direct, and fearless. In today's scripture, Jesus encounters a rich man who asks what he can
do to have eternal life. The man says he already follows
the Ten Commandments and wants to know how he can
go further in faith. Jesus answers that if he truly wants a
life of spiritual commitment, he will sacrifice everything
he has to follow Jesus. This is a hard pill to swallow, and
the man leaves, unable to give up his wealth.

Jesus exposes truth, but always in love and compassion. Jesus never spoke truth for the sake of being right
but to help illuminate shortcomings and problems so
people could find His love and guidance. Oftentimes, we,
too, can see hidden stumbling blocks in people, but if we
are led by God to bring them up them, we need to follow
Jesus's way of doing so in love.

▸ Reflection

*When you think of love, do you view truth as being part
of it? Why or why not?*

LOVE LEADS
TO HEALING

When Jesus saw him lying there and learned that he had been in this condition for a long time, he asked him, "Do you want to get well?"

John 5:6

Many people must have walked past this man, who wasn't able to walk himself, waiting by the pool of Bethesda to be healed. There may have been so many people with their own problems, in need of their own healing, that no one concerned themselves with him. But that would change the day Jesus came on the scene and noticed this man's suffering. And Jesus delivered, instantaneously healing the man.

Although we may not be able to physically heal like Jesus did, we do have the ability to help others heal through our loving kindness toward them. So many people are dealing with pain and suffering. We can help change that when we embody Jesus's lifestyle and love. You can easily help someone feel loved and seen by simply showing up for them, listening to them, or spending time with them.

▶ Activity
Look for someone who is in pain or hardship and spend some time either talking to them or bringing joy into their lives by doing something fun with them.

COMPASSIONATE LOVE

When Jesus landed and saw a large crowd, he had compassion on them, because they were like sheep without a shepherd. So he began teaching them many things.

Mark 6:34

A common thread in Jesus's ministerial life was seeing people and having compassion for them. Sometimes people look at God as being cold and judgmental primarily because of their interpretation of stories in the Old Testament. But when Jesus came, He ushered forth a new era with God, often described as the "grace covenant." Jesus is the conductor of grace and love in this world, and when He interacted with other people during His ministry, He often felt their pain and had sympathy toward them.

Jesus understood people were fundamentally lost and in need of a leader, a shepherd, a Savior. He understood the plight of humanity. Now, since He has revealed His love to us, He invites us to have the same compassion for others. To love like Jesus is to extend kindness and compassion to those around us so they can also feel Jesus's love.

▸ Prayer

Jesus, I want to embrace Your compassionate love more and more. Help me respond to others with compassion and grace. Amen.

THE GOOD
SHEPHERD

I am the good shepherd. The good shepherd lays down his life for the sheep.

John 10:11

Jesus equates love with taking care of others. In today's passage, Jesus refers to Himself as the "Good Shepherd," who protects and takes care of those who follow Him, even at the cost of His own life. We are called to embody what Jesus models here. Often, caring for others costs us something, too, whether it's money, time, or even freedom. But most of us have people that God has entrusted us to take care of. We love like Jesus by placing ourselves in the sandals of the Good Shepherd and tending to those who need us.

We may not always feel as though we have the strength to do this on our own, but if we submit ourselves to God, He will show us how to care for those around us. Remember, Jesus is always the source for what *we* need, too, as we try to display His love to others in our lives.

▸ Prayer
Spend some time in prayer asking God to reveal how He wants you to love people in your life, like the Good Shepherd does.

LOVE
ANTICIPATES NEEDS

They have already been with me three days and have nothing to eat. If I send them home hungry, they will collapse on the way, because some of them have come a long distance.

Mark 8:2-3

During the early part of Jesus's ministry, people were so captivated by His teachings and miracles that they often never left His side. At times they even neglected their basic needs for fear of missing out. Jesus, being the Good Shepherd, recognized what they needed before they asked. In these verses, He sees they are so hungry that if He sends them home, they will be too weak from malnutrition to arrive there safely.

In this story, Jesus anticipates the people's needs and provides food for them by performing a miracle, multiplying a few loaves and pieces of fish to make enough to feed a crowd of four thousand. The lesson here is not to hope for a miracle but rather to anticipate the needs of others around you to help them or show them love, just like Jesus in today's scripture. One way to step into Jesus's love is to be aware of those around you and to provide for their needs, as Jesus did.

▶ Activity

Is there someone in your life who is overworked or exhausted? Try to think of a few ways you can extend love and help to them.

LOVE THE SINNER

When they kept on questioning him, he straightened up and said to them, "Let any one of you who is without sin be the first to throw a stone at her."

John 8:7

Jesus wasn't concerned with what people thought was right or wrong, even if it pertained to the Law. The Old Testament checklists of rules and regulations overlooked the condition of a person's heart and were often hypocritical. But through Jesus, we only need faith in Him to fulfill the Law.

In today's scripture, the religious leaders are condemning a woman for adultery. According to the Law, they have the right to do so. But Jesus wasn't interested in condemning her. He reveals that those persecuting this woman are just as guilty. No one is perfect. We all have sinned in some form or another.

This is one of the primary reasons Jesus came. God knew humanity would fall short of being perfect, so He made a different way possible through Jesus. We, too, can fall into the trap of judging others' actions. But when we step into that role, we are acting like the Pharisees in this passage. We are called to love, compassion, and truth, not judgment.

▸ Reflection

How preoccupied are you with other people's actions? Are you more likely to view their failings with compassion or judgment? Reflect on this in your journal.

LETTING OTHERS LOVE YOU

"Leave her alone," Jesus replied. "It was intended that she should save this perfume for the day of my burial."

John 12:7-8

Have you ever had a hard time receiving an expensive gift? Many people do. They can feel as though it's too much, or that the money should have been spent on something else. But Jesus shows us the importance of not rejecting people's gifts. In this scripture, Mary, Lazarus's sister, has just anointed Jesus's feet with perfume. Although the apostle Judas argues that the perfume should be sold and the money given to the poor, Jesus accepts the gift instead, which is a surprising response.

We are not called to an ascetic lifestyle but a balanced existence. It's okay to receive gifts from time to time. Jesus accepts the perfume because He knows that Mary's gift is given out of pure love and adoration. Judas does not see that, nor does he care about this gift of love. It's important to recognize that when people give gifts, it's usually done as an expression of love, and whatever the gift is, it's really the giver's love that we're accepting.

▸ Reflection

What is it like for you to receive gifts? Do you ever feel as though you don't deserve them? Why or why not?

HUMBLE LOVE

After that, he poured water into a basin and began to wash his disciples' feet, drying them with the towel that was wrapped around him.

John 13:5

Humility is a prominent characteristic of Jesus. Kings are not usually known for humility, however, so when Jesus bent down and grabbed the disciples' dirt-caked feet, it was highly unusual. Jesus's love was radical and changed the way people viewed God. You see, everything Jesus did was to model what it looked like to be a person of God. God never expects us to do anything He wouldn't do or hasn't already done. To love like Jesus is to take a stance of humility and to be in service of others, all because of the love we have for God.

The idea is not to neglect ourselves through a constant lifestyle of serving others, but to be open and willing to be humble, especially when the Lord calls us to do so. Love creates the desire to put others before self, just like Jesus did.

▶ Activity

Model Jesus's love by doing something selfless this week in service to someone who is close to you.

JESUS'S LOVE BROUGHT PEOPLE TOGETHER

When Jesus saw his mother there, and the disciple whom he loved standing nearby, he said to her, "Woman, here is your son," and to the disciple, "Here is your mother."

John 19:26–27

The compassion and love Jesus consistently displayed is jaw dropping. As Jesus was dying on the cross, He stopped to take care of His mother. Understanding Mary's grief over what she was about to lose, Jesus took it upon Himself to have John become His replacement. Not only that, but John, being the youngest disciple, also would be lost without Jesus. Jesus fixed this problem and created for them a new family upon His death.

The lesson for us is that loving like Jesus means embarking on a radical new way of viewing life and people. Jesus took care of people, but always through the lens of truth and love. We, too, can take care of those around us by simply looking beneath the surface and asking God to help us love others and care for them like Jesus did.

▶ Prayer

Jesus, Your love is extraordinary! I want to be a channel of Your love to those around me. Help me see others the way You see them so I can extend Your love to all. Amen.

JESUS'S LOVE MEETS US IN OUR DOUBT

Then he said to Thomas, "Put your finger here; see my hands. Reach out your hand and put it into my side. Stop doubting and believe."

John 20:27

"Doubting Thomas" stands out every Easter season as the one who questioned whether Jesus had really risen from the dead. I've always felt sorry for Thomas, who gets a bad rap. Doesn't he simply ask what we all ask: "Are you real, Jesus?" Instead of scolding him, belittling him, or chastising him, however, Jesus instead meets Thomas in his inquiry. That's not too different from how Jesus meets us in our doubts and questions, right?

This is Jesus's love. It is safe and secure and does not falter even when we question whether Jesus can do everything He says, or if He truly is who He claims to be. Doubt doesn't scare Jesus. He meets us where we are and responds with true love and grace. To love like Jesus is to be comfortable with the way He loves us, allowing us to come to Him freely and openly with our doubts.

▶ Reflection

Where might you doubt Jesus's capabilities in your life or a situation you are facing? Journal about your findings and bring them before the Lord in prayer.

JESUS'S LOVE RESTORES

Peter was hurt because Jesus asked him the third time, "Do you love me?" He said, "Lord, you know all things; you know that I love you." Jesus said, "Feed my sheep."

John 21:17

Before Jesus died, Peter was hiding in the courtyard. When asked if he knew Jesus, Peter three times denied being a follower of Christ. Feeling low and disappointed in his cowardice, Peter knew he had messed up. After the Resurrection, Jesus and Peter had the exchange described in today's scripture. For as many times as Peter denied Jesus, Jesus restored Him with a simple question: "Peter, do you love me?"

Hurt by Jesus's inquiry, Peter completely missed what He was doing, which was restoring Peter by reminding him that his love for Jesus was still alive and would be the basis of his future ministry, despite his mistake.

Jesus's love restores. No matter how far we have fallen, His love can reach and repair us. Nothing could ever separate us from the love Jesus has for us. It was the same for Peter.

▸ Reflection

Reflect on a time when Jesus brought restoration to your life after a mistake. Write about it in your journal.

LOVE
THE OUTCAST

A man with leprosy came to him and begged him on his knees, "If you are willing, you can make me clean." Jesus was indignant. He reached out his hand and touched the man. "I am willing," he said. "Be clean!"

Mark 1:40-41

Have you ever felt too dirty, too problematic, or too far gone for Jesus to reach you?

Anyone who contracted leprosy in ancient times was considered an outcast. People feared the disease, which was thought to be highly contagious. Those with leprosy lived a terribly isolated life. Although most healthy people refused to get anywhere near a person with leprosy, Jesus reached out without hesitation, offering human contact and healing, because nobody is out of reach of His love.

But Jesus's love isn't just for us to receive; it is also for us to give. We are called to emulate this same type of compassionate love toward those who feel rejected, left out, or lonely. As Christians, we should extend love to all people, but especially those who need it most.

▶ Activity

Do you know anyone in your church or community who is lonely? Plan to connect with them and extend love to them to help them feel valued.

EXTENDING LOVE
TO THE SINNER

On hearing this, Jesus said to them, "It is not the healthy who need a doctor, but the sick. I have not come to call the righteous, but sinners."

Mark 2:17

It's easy to fall into drawing lines in the sand between "good" people and "bad." But Jesus often spent His time with the people in society who were unwanted, unpopular, lowly, cast aside, oppressed, and even hated. Jesus cared for and loved those who were judged and looked down upon. We're often drawn to those who are well liked, seem to always do the right thing, or appear to have no problems. However, our love shouldn't be reserved for the people who might be easier to love. Jesus wants us to extend it to all walks of life, as He did. Jesus didn't just come for the righteous. He came for those who were lost and needed a Savior.

Jesus calls us to see all people as worthy of our love, no matter who they are. Of course, this doesn't mean putting ourselves in unsafe situations, but it does mean having a mindset that is open to loving those who we think of as different than ourselves—whether they are or not—especially those who are hurting.

▶ Prayer
Jesus, I ask You to grow my heart to care even more for all people so I can be a vessel of Your love in this world. Help me to love those You love. Amen.

OPEN COMMUNICATION

If your brother or sister sins, go and point out their fault, just between the two of you. If they listen to you, you have won them over.

Matthew 18:15

When someone hurts us, we often fall into one of two responses. We either avoid and allow the anger to soften, or we escalate into an argument. Jesus points us to neither of these solutions but rather to a radical and healthy formula that asks us to talk openly about grievances with our offender. It's important to note that Jesus refers to siblings in the scripture, denoting a close relationship, not an interaction with a stranger. For a good outcome, speaking openly about someone's faults may require a more intimate relationship.

Being in relationships, especially close ones, can be difficult. Feelings get hurt; actions are misinterpreted. It's almost as though the closer you get to someone the more vulnerable you become. That is why Jesus encourages us to get through differences and hurt feelings by lovingly and truthfully confronting the pain that happens in our close relationships.

▶ Reflection
When you face disagreements, do you express your feelings in a way that reflects today's scripture? If not, how can you embrace Jesus's teaching the next time you are hurt?

RESOLVE CONFLICT

Therefore, if you are offering your gift at the altar and there remember that your brother or sister has something against you, leave your gift there in front of the altar. First go and be reconciled to them; then come and offer your gift.

Matthew 5:23-24

How vigilant are you about solving conflicts? For most of us, trying to resolve conflict produces stress, anxiety, fear, and caution, especially if we are on the receiving end of someone's anger. In today's passage, Jesus is directing our steps and our actions when we've hurt someone close to us.

Instead of carrying on with the normal duties of life, or in Jesus's example, bringing tithes and gifts to the church, we are called to stop what we are doing, ask for forgiveness for our wrongdoing, and work toward reconciliation, so we can then approach God with a clean heart. Loving like Jesus means acknowledging the faults in our relationships and making amends when we have done something hurtful, whether intentional or not.

Reconciliation in relationships is incredibly important to God because that's exactly what Jesus's life was for: to make amends between God and humanity.

▶ Prayer

Is there anyone in your life you have hurt from whom you need to seek forgiveness? Ask God to give you the humility, courage, and love to reach out to that person.

LOVE UNIFIES

I have given them the glory that you gave me, that they may be one as we are one—I in them and you in me—so that they may be brought to complete unity.

John 17:22-23

The culture we live in is one of division, polarizing differences, being on one side or the other. As a people, we have lost the concept of unity. But love is unifying. It sees no boundary markers, it crosses territories, and it bridges gaps. Love is Jesus, exemplified by His life. Being with the rich and the poor, the downtrodden and the elite, the grieving and the joyful, Jesus crossed social, economic, and political boundaries to bring His love to all people.

In a polarized society, it can be difficult to stand in the middle and extend love to both sides of the line. Whether people have opposing political views or raise their children in different ways, Jesus calls us to show love through unity and—of course—loving our enemies. Jesus's love unifies and bridges the gap between differing parties and beliefs.

▶ Prayer
God, help me be a person who finds commonality, not differences, with others. Help me be a bridge of love and compassion to those with whom I do not agree. Amen.

EXPRESSING
LOVE

*I have told you this so that my joy may be in you
and that your joy may be complete.*

John 15:11

Especially toward the end of His ministry, Jesus expressed
His deep love for His friends. He didn't hold His feelings
or emotions back because He wanted those He loved to
know how He felt. Sometimes we can be afraid to express
our feelings because it puts us in a vulnerable place. We
wonder what will happen if the other person doesn't
reciprocate our feelings. It can be scary to express our
emotions. But not for Jesus, whose love didn't fluctuate
according to how others received it. Jesus's love wasn't
dependent on circumstances or behavior. It was love in
the purest and truest sense.

When we allow Jesus to be the source of our love,
we are free to love in the way He modeled, without
being dependent on any contingencies. When we have
Jesus as the source of our love and allow our love to emulate His, we can feel confident in expressing our love to
others without fear of rejection.

▶ Activity

*Find a creative way to express your love to someone
in your life. Write them a note, make them a present,
surprise them with their favorite activity, or simply tell
them what they mean to you.*

ENDLESS LOVE

It was just before the Passover Festival. Jesus knew that the hour had come for him to leave this world and go to the Father. Having loved his own who were in the world, he loved them to the end.

John 13:1

Even to the very end, Jesus loved His disciples. He knew who would deny Him. He knew who would betray Him. He knew who would be there as He died. Most of His friends were afraid in His darkest moments and were not there for Jesus in the end. Still, Jesus's love for them remained.

People will always disappoint us because they are not God and are far from perfect. Humans cannot provide for us in all the ways we need because people are broken. We are all in need of a Savior. Jesus was able to love His friends even when they failed Him because He didn't rely on them as His source of strength and love. Instead, He relied on the Father to be His source for everything. This is how Jesus could love endlessly, and it is a model for us to follow. Allowing God to become everything for us enables us to have love like Jesus and accept others' shortcomings.

▶ Reflection
Spend time reflecting on what it feels like to be disappointed by others, and contrast that with the dependability of God. How does God's love fill you in ways nothing else can?

PARENTAL LOVE

Or if he asks for an egg, will you give him a scorpion? If you then, though you are evil, know how to give good gifts to your children, how much more will your Father in heaven give the Holy Spirit to those who ask him!

Luke 11:12-13

Oftentimes we can confuse God's love with our parents' love. If we weren't raised in a safe, loving home, we may not feel we can trust God as our Father.

The truth is that no one out there has had a perfect human parent. Such a thing doesn't exist. Even if the people who raised us were wonderful, they probably still made mistakes, some of which likely affected us in negative ways. Others of us have more difficult issues to navigate when thinking about their upbringing. Our caregivers were not God. They didn't have all the answers, and in some cases their love may have been very flawed.

Whether our parents were saints or our childhoods were challenging, the way we were raised does not equate with God's parental love. God the Father's love is perfect, supreme, exemplary, and faultless. His love heals, restores, and brings hope. Although the love in our childhood may have had flaws, God the Father's love is exactly what we need every moment of every day.

▶ Reflection

Recall your thoughts and emotions about your upbringing. Are they positive, negative, indifferent? How might your feelings about your earthly caregivers reflect on your thoughts about God as your perfect parent?

JESUS'S LOVE CHANGES OUR FUTURE

I no longer call you servants, because a servant does not know his master's business. Instead, I have called you friends.

John 15:15

Before becoming a follower of Jesus, I was headed down a troubled and dangerous path. But like many Christians, Jesus radically changed my situation in life, forever altering my future. Because of Jesus's love, I have been made anew and I have been elevated to a new status in life, as a child of God and a friend of Jesus.

Jesus's love changes our future. Jesus shapes our identity. He elevates us to new places, giving us newness simply because we follow Him and He loves us. This doesn't only happen at conversion, though. Jesus's love continually changes us and propels us forward, as it did with His disciples. The closer to Jesus we get, the more we follow His teachings and allow Him to be the center of our lives, the more we grow into His likeness.

▶ Prayer

Jesus, thank You for restoring, redeeming, and altering my future. I am a new creation with a hopeful future because of You. Amen.

OTHER
CHRISTIANS ARE FAMILY

Someone told him, "Your mother and brothers are standing outside, wanting to see you." He replied, "My mother and brothers are those who hear God's word and put it into practice."

Luke 8:20-21

One thing I love dearly about being a Christian is having instant family wherever there are other Christians around. There is a likeness and commonality among believers that creates bonds quickly, and there is a comfort in finding fellowship with people who also love Jesus and are living out His values of kindness, love, mercy, and compassion. It helps us on our own faith journey to see others working to become more like Him.

So whether you have a robust family or no family at all, whenever you encounter another Christian, you are among family. God knows we are created for relationships, and if we ask Him for this connection, He will lovingly provide us with a network of people who will love and support us in our faith. Furthermore, this is much like how it will be when we get to Heaven: full of support and devoid of loneliness.

▶ Reflection

Think back on all the spiritual relationships and connections you have made with others. Thank God for how He has brought these people into your life.

LOVE THE LEAST AMONG YOU

Whoever welcomes this little child in my name welcomes me; and whoever welcomes me welcomes the one who sent me. For it is the one who is least among you all who is the greatest.

Luke 9:48

Compared with adults, children have very few responsibilities or rights. Although some children are forced to grow up at earlier ages, kids are not running the country; they are not even usually in charge of when they go to bed. A child's life typically means being required to follow directions and eventually growing up to have more independence and the ability to choose what they want for dinner.

Although many people romanticize childhood, from a kid's perspective it can feel disempowering. They must seek permission for most things and are generally not treated as equals. This is all important to hold in tension as we read today's scripture.

Jesus asks us to look out for the powerless, for those who need guidance and protection. He calls us to view those who are perceived to be least in our society as the greatest, to value simplicity and humility in ourselves and in others. Jesus's love is countercultural in what it values. He calls us to emulate that love to the least among us.

▸ Activity

Reflect on this scripture or spend some time with a child in your life, if you have one. Try to appreciate the qualities in them that Jesus would value.

PRAYER IS AN EXPRESSION OF LOVE

Righteous Father, though the world does not know you, I know you, and they know that you have sent me. I have made you known to them, and will continue to make you known in order that the love you have for me may be in them and that I myself may be in them.

John 17:25–26

Just before Jesus was arrested, He prayed a powerful prayer that wasn't just for His followers but for us here and now. Yes, in the last hours of His life, Jesus prayed for you and me. Jesus's love is so deep that it began two thousand years ago and is still active to this day.

Prayer is a powerful expression of love, and that love drips into the prayerful words of Jesus in today's scripture. When we pray, we also enter a language of love. And we direct that love toward God when we turn to Him in prayer. The more we pray for others, the more we learn to love them. And because prayers are timeless, our love is catapulted into the future as our prayers are heard by our eternal God. They have life beyond our own, as displayed in the Bible passage for today.

▶ Prayer

Jesus, thank You for praying lovingly for me two thousand years ago. I am in awe of how Your love carries through generation after generation. Amen.

▶ LOOK TO JESUS

The scriptures in parts 1 and 2 are taken from the Gospels, primarily Jesus's words, known by many Christians as the "red letters" of the text because of the color font used in printed Bibles. These sections dive deeply into Jesus's own words and His encounters with people through His ministry. Part 3 also incorporates writings from the New Testament authors who ministered after Jesus's ascension to Heaven, to see how they processed and applied Jesus's message. This section demonstrates how they looked to Jesus in their own lives and in the formation of the burgeoning church.

By combining the writings from the New Testament letters with Jesus's own words, you will begin to see how Jesus meets us now, post-Ascension, and how His truth and love penetrate to this very day two thousand years later. There isn't a scenario in our lives that Jesus cannot reach. We will unlock all of that in this final section.

WHY DO WE LOOK FOR JESUS?

You are looking for me, not because you saw the signs I performed but because you ate the loaves and had your fill.

John 6:26

Jesus's many miracles and healings drove a lot of buzz and excitement to His endeavors. Whereas some people followed Him because they were drawn to His teachings and believed He was the Son of God, others followed simply for the spectacle.

Life was difficult in Jesus's time. Most people earned a small wage for long days of hard labor. There were none of the modern distractions or accommodations that today we probably couldn't imagine living life without. So when someone started providing enough food for thousands of people from just a few fish and loaves, the people came flocking!

Jesus knew most of the people who followed Him were not interested in the nourishment of His words but rather in the food He provided. So when they sought Him out, He asked a truth-cutting question to reveal their true motivations. Jesus asks us the same question: Do we seek Him for the miracles or because He is the only way?

▶ Reflection

Why do you look for Jesus? Reflect on your motivations for seeking Jesus, and talk to God about your findings.

FINDING
RESILIENCE

But the fruit of the Spirit is love, joy, peace, for-bearance, kindness, goodness, faithfulness, gentleness and self-control. Against such things there is no law.

Galatians 5:22-23

Do you want to know the way to resilience? It's through nurturing the fruit of the Spirit. This fruit is not plural, but one, singular fruit. Believers don't receive just one of the fruits; it is God's intention to grow the fullness of the fruit into each believer's life, so we all are equipped with love, joy, peace, patience, kindness, goodness, faithfulness, gentleness, and self-control. Through the fruit of the Spirit we walk like Jesus and gain resilience to endure what life throws our way.

Resilience isn't reserved for just certain types of people; it is available to you through Jesus. If you look to Jesus as the solution to anything you face in life, He will show up, begin transforming you into His likeness, and grow His virtues of fruit in your life. Resilience is yours for the taking. Just look to Jesus.

▶ Reflection
Imagine your life with the fullness of the fruit of the Spirit. Envision how each fruit might help you not only during hardships but also in everyday life.

JESUS IS
JUST LIKE US

For we do not have a high priest who is unable to empathize with our weaknesses, but we have one who has been tempted in every way, just as we are—yet he did not sin.

Hebrews 4:15

Jesus was just like you and me, except He was also God, and He never sinned. On Earth, Jesus stripped Himself of His divine powers and depended completely on the Spirit to do all that He accomplished. But Jesus was no different from us. When we look to Jesus, we can see a perfect version of ourselves. In Jesus we find someone who came to show us what it looks like to walk with God here on Earth. Jesus has the answers to every situation in life because He's already faced anything we may go through.

Because of this, we can have confidence that Jesus knows the way through any hardship. He endured suffering, mockery, harassment, and persecution. The answer in every single situation in life is Jesus. So look to Jesus—He is the way!

▶ Reflection

How do you look to Jesus in your fears, troubles, joys, celebrations, career, dreams, and future? How can you create connections to Jesus in these areas of your life? Write in your journal.

DEALING WITH TEMPTATION

Jesus, full of the Holy Spirit, left the Jordan and was led by the Spirit into the wilderness, where for forty days he was tempted by the devil. He ate nothing during those days, and at the end of them he was hungry.

Luke 4:1-2

The temptation of Jesus is a paramount story in scripture because it helps us really see Jesus's humanity and His dependency on the Holy Spirit to provide endurance. As shown in the previous devotion, Jesus is just like us, but without sin. This story shows us the agony and hardship He went through as He was tempted at His weakest point.

Temptations are always hard to deal with. They can involve anything from battling addictions to fighting off a sugar craving to the desire to take things that don't belong to us. Yet Jesus shows us that the Holy Spirit can bring us the fruit of self-control. Jesus was enabled for success in the desert because He stood on solid and firm ground, rooted in God. The Lord is willing and able to bring us through the temptations we face. As we seek Him and ask Him to grow these virtues in us, we will be better equipped to meet temptation, just like Jesus did.

▶ Reflection
What temptations are you currently struggling with, and how can God help you with them?

REST IN JESUS

*Come to me, all you who are weary and burdened,
and I will give you rest.*

Matthew 11:28

Sometimes we can be terribly weighed down with the
pressures, worries, responsibilities, and fears that come
with being an adult. We tire even faster when we are burdened, just like a person walking up a hill empty-handed
moves more easily than one who carries a heavy load.
Burdens are cumbersome and exhausting.

Jesus was always concerned that people took care of
themselves properly and had enough nourishment and
rest. The tender care of the Good Shepherd is often unlike
the care we extend to ourselves.

God can handle whatever is weighing you down.
Your burdens will never be too heavy for Him. Jesus calls
each of us to allow ourselves to be loved and taken care
of by Him.

▶ Activity

*Come up with a list of ways you can rest in Jesus. For
example, you could create time this week where you
purposefully connect to Jesus, resting in His presence
through prayer and/or journaling.*

JESUS EQUIPS YOU

Then Jesus asked them, "When I sent you without purse, bag or sandals, did you lack anything?" "Nothing," they answered.

Luke 22:35

I don't know about you, but I like to be prepared. When going on a trip, I always overpack, as I envision scenarios that probably won't happen and uses for things that are unlikely to be needed, but I take them just in case. We are creatures of preparation, and if you are an over-packer like me, you may spend your entire life preparing for something to come. For example, most of childhood is simply trying to prepare to be an adult, as we work to gather the tools, knowledge, and skills needed to survive. However, this natural and essential rhythm in life can be hazardous to our dependence on Christ because the independence necessary to become a successful and viable adult can lead to the false belief that we can handle everything on our own.

Although we do need to learn certain skills and autonomy to survive and thrive, we also need to learn what dependency on Christ looks like and trust Him to provide for us. As we learn to entrust our burdens to the Lord, we find ourselves freer and less weighed down with the demands in our lives.

▶ Prayer

Jesus, help me rely on You for all my needs. Grow my trust that You will provide for me. Amen.

FIGHTING ANXIETY

Do not be anxious about anything, but in every situation, by prayer and petition, with thanksgiving, present your requests to God.

Philippians 4:6

Anxiety is just plain awful. The constant swirling of the stomach, the restless mind, and the quickened breath all are cumbersome conditions that dramatically impede one's life. Anxiety is very common, and although it doesn't simply go away with a prayer, there is a bit of hope found in Paul's words here.

A great strategy for combating anxiety is to recognize that God is always with us and that whatever we fear can be taken to Him. As we pray, we also have the opportunity to change our perspective and practice focusing on some good things that are occurring in our lives. Turning to praise and gratitude for God and the ways He provides for us will help broaden our perspective and can loosen the grip of anxiety. Although it will probably take much practice, each time you turn to the Lord in this way you are actively fighting anxiety. Hope is on the horizon.

▶ *Activity*
Write in your journal some comforting truths about how God provides for us and refer to them the next time you feel anxious. Use some of the scripture in this devotional as your guide.

IT'S GOOD TO BE WEAK

He said to me, "My grace is sufficient for you, for my power is made perfect in weakness." Therefore I will boast all the more gladly about my weaknesses, so that Christ's power may rest on me.

2 Corinthians 12:9

It's almost unnatural to embrace weakness. Our innate abilities, our survival instincts, have been created so we can overcome and persevere. We live in a world with hazards around every corner. But our bodies have expiration dates. We can survive for only so long, and we can't evade every problem or threat. Let's face it: We are weak and not immortal. This is why Paul's words about Jesus are important for us. We all have weaknesses. By our very nature, to be human—mortal—is to be weak. The good news is that we have a Savior who is everlasting, eternal, and capable of anything and everything, even overcoming death itself.

When we can embrace our weaknesses, whatever they may be, we can face reality and find true solutions. Our weakness enables us to tether ourselves to Christ and allow His power to reach our vulnerability. In God, our weakness makes us strong.

▶ Activity

Identify a weak area in your life. Write a prayer to the Lord addressing the weakness in your life that you want to give over to God.

VIRTUOUS TOOLS

For the Spirit God gave us does not make us timid,
but gives us power, love and self-discipline.

2 Timothy 1:7

The Lord gives us all the tools we need to be able to navigate through this often-difficult world. These tools are not human made, and we cannot purchase them. Instead, they are everlasting gifts from God. They are the same tools Jesus used in His ministry, and they were the virtues that enabled Him to change the world and endure the suffering He did.

When we depend on Jesus and look to Him as the way through life, we start to provide room for Him to build His virtues in us. The Lord lends us His strength when we are weak and cultivates His love within us, which enables us to feel secure and safe. Furthermore, He helps us build self-discipline, which enables us to achieve success. These tools are invaluable for anyone, but especially those trying to walk in line with Jesus.

God offers us the same tools Jesus had, but it's up to us to seek them, not just once but every day. The Lord will develop the virtues of power, love, and self-discipline in you so that you can face anything. Then you can overcome and stand strong because you're standing in God's strength.

▶ Reflection
Of the three virtuous tools Timothy lists, which one do you need Jesus to develop most in your life and why?

MAKING TOUGH DECISIONS

I am torn between the two: I desire to depart and be with Christ, which is better by far; but it is more necessary for you that I remain in the body.

Philippians 1:23-24

Making decisions is not easy for me. Whether it's what meal to order at a restaurant or a big life change, decisions tend to overwhelm me and cause anxiety, as I fear making the wrong choice. Making a decision is a bit of a gamble because we never know what the outcome will really be. Honestly, one way to combat prolonged decision-making is to recognize that no matter what we choose, God will be with us and see us through.

Because we do not have the whole perspective, we cannot see all the variables and outcomes of our decisions. But we can ask God to provide for us. Through prayer and support from others, we can find ways to make wise and confident decisions, knowing that God will fill in the gaps as we trust Him to pave a way forward.

▶ Prayer
Jesus, help me discern Your direction in making decisions, especially difficult ones. Please bring Your assurance, guidance, and peace as I seek the right path. Amen.

DEALING WITH DIFFICULT PEOPLE

When Jesus went outside, the Pharisees and the teachers of the law began to oppose him fiercely and to besiege him with questions, waiting to catch him in something he might say.

Luke 11:53–54

Jesus's ministry was surrounded by difficult people. He was constantly challenged, doubted, and harassed by naysayers. He seemed to have trolls around Him all the time, and yet it never stopped His mission or made Jesus feel sorry for Himself. Why? He didn't allow the difficult people, those who were trying to cause Him harm, to have any credence. Nothing they said shook Him or made Him rethink His value or validity.

For some reason, there is a subversive thought in Christianity that Jesus accepted everyone's behavior. Yet, we see Him constantly questioning the Pharisees and the religious leaders as they relentlessly attacked His character and worth. Jesus wasn't trying to win them over; He was standing up to them in truth, giving honor to God. Looking to Jesus when dealing with naysayers or difficult people means standing up for truth and not allowing your character to be drained by people who are trying to harm you.

▶ Reflection

How do you deal with difficult people? Do you avoid them, try to win them over, experience feelings of trauma? Journal about your findings and take them to the Lord in prayer.

JESUS KNOWS WHAT YOU ARE GOING THROUGH

Satan has asked to sift all of you as wheat. But I have prayed for you, Simon, that your faith may not fail. And when you have turned back, strengthen your brothers.

Luke 22:31–32

Jesus knows that hardship you may be facing. He already knows what is going to happen. In today's scripture, Jesus is aware that Satan has been chasing Simon Peter. If Peter had not been tested, would he have ever grown into the person he became? Doubtful.

Hardships are, by definition, awful and agonizing. But it is often through our hardships that we grow and achieve altitudes we wouldn't have reached otherwise.

Like an athlete training to become stronger, we have many chances to grow. But we sometimes don't see hardships for what they are. We only view them as painful, not fruit producing, Christ-character building. If we start to change perspective, we can use our difficulties to grow and become more like Jesus and embrace them as a way to grow stronger.

▶ Prayer

Jesus, help me see that what I face isn't indicative of Your lack of love in my life, but rather that You may be preparing me for something bigger, just like You did with Peter. Amen.

93

MEASURING YOUR WORTH

He asked them, "What were you arguing about on the road?" But they kept quiet because on the way they had argued about who was the greatest.

Mark 9:33–34

Pride is often a clever smokescreen for feelings of insecurity. When we begin to measure our worth against other people's successes, we find ourselves in an unending cycle of defeat. The disciples faced this same predicament and measured their worth based on future status, arguing about who would be the greatest. Of course, none of them was going to be the greatest because that title is reserved for Jesus.

Jesus wasn't at all impressed with the disciples' presumptions of importance, and He questioned why they were arguing. Of course, none of the disciples confessed because they knew they were in the wrong.

The world we live in favors some and disfavors others, sometimes for no perceivable reasons. However, when we look to Jesus, we see that the way the world operates and how it measures worth is not the same way Jesus assigns value. Your worth comes from Jesus, and Him alone, not by measuring your success against another.

▶ Reflection
Evaluate your self-worth. What builds you up and what tears you down? How much of your worth comes from Jesus?

FACING INSECURITIES

Such confidence we have through Christ before God. Not that we are competent in ourselves to claim anything for ourselves, but our competence comes from God.

2 Corinthians 3:4-5

Most people struggle from time to time with feeling insecure. Even though insecurity is a common and natural feeling, if left unchecked it can hold us back from the person God is calling us to be. Can you imagine how ineffective Jesus would have been if He were insecure? Would He have been able to reach as many people or stand up in God's truth against His accusers? Probably not. This is why, when we face insecurity, we can look to Jesus for answers.

Jesus was able to stand firm in the truth of God because His competence came directly from His Father. Because Jesus was solid in God, insecurity did not creep up in His life. We grow in security, as Jesus did, when we rely on God's strength to fill up our confidence. When insecurity rises within us, we can turn to Jesus's words to speak truth into our lives.

▸ Activity

Make a list of your insecurities. Next to each item on that list, write, "Jesus gives me confidence."

NAVIGATING TRANSITIONS

After he said this, he was taken up before their very eyes, and a cloud hid him from their sight.

Acts 1:9

Can you imagine what difficult transitions these events were for Jesus's first disciples? To have watched Him die, come back to life, and then ascend to Heaven before their very eyes? After they had lived with Jesus for three years and stayed by His side for everything, He was suddenly gone. What would they do? I think we all can find commonality with today's scripture. We, too, have navigated transitions that have left us baffled, directionless, and unsure of how to proceed.

What Jesus told the disciples right before He left was critical for them, as it is for us as we navigate transitions in life. Jesus told them He was leaving the Holy Spirit with them and that they would never be alone. When we need to move forward, to traverse intimidating paths, let's remember we are never on our own. The Spirit of the Lord is always with us, guiding us through the unknown terrain.

▶ Prayer

Jesus, help me embrace transitions knowing You have provided the Holy Spirit to be my guide. Although I cannot see everything, You can. Help me trust in Your guidance. Amen.

WHAT ARE
YOU THINKING ABOUT?

*Finally, brothers and sisters, whatever is true,
whatever is noble, whatever is right, whatever is
pure, whatever is lovely, whatever is admirable—if
anything is excellent or praiseworthy—think about
such things.*

Philippians 4:8

You truly are what you think about. Our thoughts inform
our actions and direct our lives. The more healthy and
holy our thoughts are, the more peace and joy we can
find. If our thoughts are always shaped by worry, anxiety,
stress, and fear, then our lives will reflect disharmony, irri-
tability, and possibly even disdain. Furthermore, if we are
wrapped up in thoughts of unfairness, bitterness, or even
anger, our actions will mirror those thoughts.

When we look to Jesus, we can ask ourselves, "Would
Jesus think about such things?" If you can't imagine Jesus
giving certain thoughts much time or energy, ask yourself
why you are dwelling on such matters. Instead, let us walk
in harmony with Paul's suggestion today to think about
noble, right, pure, lovely, admirable, praiseworthy things.
Fill your thoughts with positive, truthful ideas and you
will follow in the way Jesus thought.

▶ Activity
*For the next twenty-four hours, jot down the things you're
thinking about. After you finish, see if your thoughts
reveal any patterns.*

YOU CAN
DO THINGS IN CHRIST

I can do all this through him who gives me strength.

Philippians 4:13

Many of us have scripts in our head about the things we believe we are not capable of doing. In a sense, we lie to ourselves about things we are scared to do or that intimidate us. Yet, we have the unfailing word of God that beckons us to think differently. In today's scripture, Paul points the reader to his life and how he was able to overcome enormous feats and suffering, all because of Christ, who gave him the strength and endurance.

This wasn't just true for Paul's first readers; it applies to us here and now. There is nothing we will ever face without God's presence offering His strength, guidance, support, and love. He equips us strongly, and the more we lean on Him, the stronger and more secure in Him we become.

The Lord will strengthen you and equip you to get through any hardship, for He is good, loyal, and loving.

▶ Prayer
Jesus, help me see Your strength in my life so I can face whatever the world throws my way. When I feel shaky and weak, please come to my rescue. Amen.

GRIEVING
LIKE JESUS

"Where have you laid him?" he asked. "Come and see, Lord," they replied. Jesus wept. Then the Jews said, "See how he loved him!"

John 11:34-36

Today's scripture is of utmost importance to understand the humanity of Jesus and how He experienced all the emotions we feel. Losing someone is hard, and the natural response is to mourn the loss, to desire for your loved one to be back alive and with you. It feels unfair, too much to bear at times, but we can find comfort in our Savior who healthily displayed emotions at the loss of His friend Lazarus. Even though He would raise Lazarus from the dead shortly afterward, the snapshot of Jesus's tears, His weeping, is what catches our attention here.

Whereas outward expressions of grief come naturally for some, others have a hard time giving themselves permission to grieve. Sometimes it makes us feel weak, but there is no weakness in grieving. It is healthy and necessary for us to cope and move on. One day there will be no more tears and no more crying, and we look forward to that day in Heaven.

▸ Activity
Read the story of the death and resurrection of Lazarus in John 11:1–44. Take note of any feelings or thoughts that come forward and bring them to God in prayer.

THE PULL

No one can serve two masters. Either you will hate the one and love the other, or you will be devoted to the one and despise the other. You cannot serve both God and money.

Matthew 6:24

In today's scripture, Jesus explains the pull between following God and following money. It can be easy to dismiss the idea of the pull of money, but money is sneaky and slippery and can take us captive without us noticing. We need it for even the necessities of food, water, shelter, electricity, and transportation.

Because money is intrinsically woven into the fabric of our lives, it's important to be aware of how much we need it to survive. But Jesus's teaching is intended to help us uncover hidden motivators and the influence and pressure money brings.

By allowing God to be the one you follow, you naturally eradicate the demands money can place on you. God can help reshape your desires and spending habits and bring restoration and guidance where finances are problematic. Often, we spend money on things we think will bring us happiness, but when God is the source of joy, there's nothing money can buy to bring us the contentment we find in Him. Jesus knew money wouldn't solve His problems, but God would.

▶ Prayer
Lord, I want to follow You and not be swayed or consumed by money. Let me love You first and help me trust that You will provide for me. Amen.

DON'T WORK YOURSELF TOO HARD

Then, because so many people were coming and going that they did not even have a chance to eat, he said to them, "Come with me by yourselves to a quiet place and get some rest."

Mark 6:31

It would be natural to think the disciples shouldn't rest or find time for breaks because Jesus's ministry was only three years old and had a serious objective. There was so much need, so many people in need of healing and desperate to get near the Messiah. Amid all that popularity, Jesus put things in the proper order by calling His disciples to stop and not work too hard.

Jesus wants us to be taken care of, to be fully charged so that we can be a true vessel of His light, love, and truth in the world. God is capable of everything and is in control of the entire cosmos. Sometimes we lose perspective and think we're responsible for everything and that there is no time to stop. When we operate like that we are working in our own strength and not taking care of ourselves. But Jesus's call is for us not to work so hard that we neglect our own needs.

▸ Activity

Do you find yourself working yourself too hard? Make a list of five ways you can scale back and tend to your own needs.

THE FRUIT OF TRUSTING JESUS

*May the God of hope fill you with all joy and peace
as you trust in him, so that you may overflow with
hope by the power of the Holy Spirit.*

Romans 15:13

No matter what problems we face, the solution is always
Jesus. When you are deeply tied to Jesus, a new frame-
work begins to emerge in your life. Trust builds as Jesus
becomes a daily companion. You begin to see how God
moves and works all things together for your good. Every
time you lean on God, more trust is built, so that eventually trust in God is your default position.

This is vital because life is difficult, and we need God's
help constantly. The more trust that develops, the more
we can release the stressors in our life and relax into the
Lord's good and capable arms. Therefore, we will also be
blessed with peace and joy—something that is hard to
come by. People crave these things and try to meet those
needs in so many ways, yet they only come consistently
through an ongoing relationship with Jesus, trusting Him
always as your guide.

▶ Reflection
*Evaluate your trust in Jesus. How well do you trust Jesus
in hardships? Relationship problems? Illness? Your everyday life? Take your findings to the Lord in prayer.*

PERSEVERANCE

Blessed is the one who perseveres under trial because, having stood the test, that person will receive the crown of life that the Lord has promised to those who love him.

James 1:12

To persevere means to have persistence throughout difficult situations or trials. It means not quitting even when things become difficult. Grit and perseverance are sometimes lost in today's way of thinking. When the going gets tough, many people get going. But as Christians, we are called to persevere through the hardship because we can endure all things through Christ who gives us strength and reminds us that we never fight battles alone.

Although some situations do require us to walk away, other times we find ourselves in a scenario that has no escape plan. Illnesses, unrealized dreams, disabilities— these all require perseverance. We simply cannot just wish the suffering away or pray that a dramatic miracle will spare us every time. Although we always can, and should, pray to God for healing, we also need to turn to God to equip and strengthen us to persevere during our trials. He will help us in anything we are going through.

▶ Prayer
Lord, help me seek Your perseverance whenever I face a trial. Help me feel Your presence and strength equipping me for the road ahead. Amen.

WHEN BAD THINGS HAPPEN

Be joyful in hope, patient in affliction, faithful in prayer.

Romans 12:12

Sometimes bad things happen because we live in a broken world. Following Jesus doesn't mean we will be sheltered from all of life's hardships. Part of being in this world means facing trials. We are not in Heaven yet; this world is still broken, and we are living in perishing bodies. The more we step into the reality that bad things will happen, the more we can be prepared for those days.

A major part of Jesus coming to this earth was to show us that no matter what happens, God will lend His strength and guidance to us. This is part of His protection, His hand over our lives, and this is how we can find joyful hope and patience when we face difficulties or unexpected trials. When bad things happen, reflect on God's presence with you always. Focusing on what God can do will help produce hope and patient endurance while you stand in faithful prayer, seeking His guidance and strength for whatever you face.

▶ Activity

On a sheet of paper, make three columns with the headings "Hope," "Patience," and "Prayer." In the "Hope" column, write down your greatest desires. Then, in the "Patience" and "Prayer" columns, describe what waiting for each looks like and how you can pursue it in prayer.

UNFULFILLED DREAMS

*Now faith is confidence in what we hope for and
assurance about what we do not see.*

The older we become, the more we realize life often takes
us on paths we never expected to travel. Because life is
often unpredictable, our dreams can suffer or stay unrealized. Perhaps you have found yourself reflecting on a
lost dream, or maybe you are regretful about or grieving
something you still desire.

So much of scripture tells of God's people longing for
something. Longing for the promised land, a king, their
homeland, the Messiah, and now—today—for the Messiah
to return so we can live in paradise with Him.

One lens through which to view ourselves as Christians
is as people who can patiently endure. We can find comfort in scripture by recognizing that we all deeply wish
for things that have not yet come to pass. Our unfulfilled
dreams can be met with a hope that comes from knowing God has always heard the desires of His people and
provided. God does have a plan for your dreams, but you
might need to wait in order to see them become reality.

▸ Activity
*Read Hebrews 11 and notice the impressive list of faith-
ful people of God who waited for their dreams and for
God's plans to come to fruition. Afterward, speak to the
Lord about acquiring patient faith as you work toward
your dreams.*

RELATIONSHIP WOES

Above all, love each other deeply, because love covers over a multitude of sins.

1 Peter 4:8

Relationships are hard because it takes determination and dedication to have a long-lasting and meaningful connection. Relationships do not come easily or effortlessly; they require a lot of work. Often, we tend to focus on the other person's problems or what we think they're doing wrong, but, as you've probably heard many times, you can only change yourself. That's something we can often forget in our relationships.

It is impossible to change anyone; only God can do that. So what do you do when you have a dispute, an argument, or a deep hurt form in a relationship? You turn to the Lord and ask Him to help you work on yourself and love the other person like God loves all people. This is a healthy way to deal with certain problems that only you can work on. Lean on God to help you find a way forward with the other person.

▶ Prayer
Lord, other people may let me down, but You are perfect and complete. Help me draw all my strength and ability to love from You and focus on my own issues rather than on others' shortcomings. Amen.

FINDING
YOUR PEOPLE

*They broke bread in their homes and ate together
with glad and sincere hearts, praising God and
enjoying the favor of all the people.*

Acts 2:46-47

Are you longing for supportive friends or community?
Do you find yourself wishing for deeper connections
and fellowship? The earliest Christians, the church after
Jesus ascended to Heaven, lived close to one another and
became like family. In that time, God worked mightily and
powerfully among them. When we find real relationships
with others who are seeking after Jesus first—building
each other up and emphasizing God's ideals of kindness,
mercy, and acceptance—it helps us do the same.

Strong friendships like these fortify us and help us
grow more Christlike virtues in our lives. When we sur-
round ourselves with others who are following Christ, it
helps hold us accountable for our own beliefs and actions.

If you don't yet have people like this in your life, ask
God to send them to you. When you find your people, the
Lord works more profoundly and prominently in your life
because His presence is magnified through the people
around you.

▶ Reflection

*Look at the close people in your life. What have they
brought to your life? How has God grown you through
them? Write in your journal.*

HOW TO KNOW
GOD'S WILL FOR YOU

*Do not conform to the pattern of this world, but be
transformed by the renewing of your mind. Then
you will be able to test and approve what God's will
is—his good, pleasing and perfect will.*

Romans 12:2

Have you ever wondered about what God wants you to
do? What path you should pursue or what decision you
should make? I sure have been in that spot many times.
In many cases, God's answer wasn't always obvious and
required stepping out in faith and asking God to show me
the best way forward. I once spoke to a spiritual advisor
who told me, "There is no wrong decision in life as long
as it adheres to the principles and governance of God."

In other words, making a decision when you want
God's will to be done doesn't have to be difficult. You
simply need to measure your options, and so long as
your choices are not harmful or disobedient to God, it's a
quality decision. If Jesus would do it, it is probably a good
choice to make. On the other hand, if Jesus wouldn't do
it, that's a strong indication that it probably isn't a good
decision.

▶ Reflection
*Reflect on your decision-making process. How often do
you seek God's will when you make a decision?*

ALLEVIATING FEAR

So we say with confidence, "The Lord is my helper; I will not be afraid. What can mere mortals to do me?"

Hebrews 13:6

Fear simply cannot be wished away. It is unlikely that God will miraculously and instantaneously heal you from fear. Rather, overcoming fear takes a lot of practice and intentionality. Fear can be conquered with God, but it's not as easy as it might seem because God conquers fear in your life by rewiring your thoughts and helping you create new patterns of behavior.

The more you believe God is your helper, that He is on your side, that He wants only good for you, the less you will become afraid. Then you will begin to develop new ways to approach situations that eventually help alleviate fear. Furthermore, a lot of fear is found in our feelings when we try to escape pain or avoid facing something. This is where God really steps in. He never leaves us, He is always with us, and He will go with us through any hardship while lending His power and support to help us find resilience.

▸ Prayer

God, thank You for always being with me, even in my fear. I want to find Your peace and strength to face anything. Help me grow in my trust of You. Amen.

HOW TO DEAL WITH CONFRONTATION

Do not let any unwholesome talk come out of your mouths, but only what is helpful for building others up according to their needs, that it may benefit those who listen.

Ephesians 4:29

Sometimes things need to be confronted and aired out. However, the way we speak to others matters to God. Jesus handled this masterfully throughout His entire ministry, especially when He confronted His naysayers and accusers.

This scripture teaches us that our speech matters. Although we cannot control other people and how they receive our words, we can manage how we convey our grievances and concerns. Our intention should never be to repay evil with evil but rather to share our feelings and thoughts with the purpose of repairing and restoring, and for the sake of love. We often have confrontations because we feel there has been an injustice, but how often do we seek confrontation for wholeness instead of spite or expressing anger? Jesus confronted others to bring them His truth and love, and we should follow His example when we need to air things out.

▶ Reflection

Do you feel comfortable confronting others, or do you find yourself only confronting situations when you are very angry? How do you think God wants you to handle these issues in relationships?

LIVING JOYFULLY

For the joy set before him he endured the cross, scorning its shame, and sat down at the right hand of the throne of God.

Hebrews 12:2

Joy is not happiness. Instead, joy is a fruit of the Spirit; it is not dependent on circumstances. Happiness comes from temporary situations, such as eating ice cream or attending a celebration. Joy comes from being truly content in Jesus and being thankful that God is with us always and providing for us. Joy is internal. It's the result of our connection to God, of living in a state of gratitude.

Living joyfully in Jesus is a life pursuit. It is a journey that requires us to pray to God and ask Him to develop the fruit of joy in us. We grow joy in our lives by being dedicated to making Jesus and His ways our top priority. As Jesus becomes more important in our lives and we follow His teachings diligently, we will see not only joy form, but many other amazing Christlike virtues as well. Joy is ours for the taking! Our admission ticket is to keep close to Jesus and seek after Him in all that we do.

▶ Reflection

How has your concept of joy changed as you've grown in your faith? How has following Jesus brought you joy?

GROWING
IN PATIENCE

Therefore, as God's chosen people, holy and dearly loved, clothe yourselves with compassion, kindness, humility, gentleness and patience.

Colossians 3:12

In a world of instant access, we are rapidly losing the art of patience, which is a very dangerous thing to lose. Without patience, people are quick to anger. They live in a false reality of immediacy. Of course, it's nice to have television shows that stream instantly and services that bring food right to our door, but with such comforts and instant access to things, we start to lower our tolerance for waiting. And whether we like it or not, we must wait for many things in life. The most important things do not come quickly. Even suffering itself requires a form of patient endurance.

If we do not have any practice waiting for things that are easy, how will we ever have endurance in hardship or the patience to cope when things are difficult? This is why it is crucial that we follow the wisdom in scripture and practice patience. It is a virtue we need in order to live well and be like Jesus in this world.

▶ Prayer
Jesus, I seek to have the kind of patience that only comes from You. Please grow the fruit of patience in my life. Amen.

LIVING COUNTERCULTURALLY

For the grace of God has appeared that offers salvation to all people. It teaches us to say "No" to ungodliness and worldly passions, and to live self-controlled, upright and godly lives in this present age.

Titus 2:11–12

The whole message of Jesus points us to live counterculturally. Fame, fortune, and success are the great enchantments of this world; sometimes it seems like its motto is dog eat dog. Yet Jesus calls us to a different life, one where we live with humility and repay evil with mercy. Jesus's message is not for the proud but rather for those who are open for real transformation and a life of true fulfillment in God.

To follow Jesus means to pursue spiritual strength rather than chasing worldly success, monetary pursuits, or even social media likes. As we live in this world, rather than subscribing to all its values, we are called to follow God's way and be His light in it.

▶ Reflection

Do you think your faith has led you to live differently than others? Can you define ways your values reflect Jesus in your life?

HANDLING CRITICISM

See what great love the Father has lavished on us, that we should be called children of God! And that is what we are! The reason the world does not know us is that it did not know him.

1 John 3:1

For some people, criticism slides right off. For others, criticism replays in the mind like a broken record. It can be hard to let go of what people have said to us or about us. Words, despite their intention, can truly sting. One way to handle criticism is to remember who you are in Christ.

People will always have an opinion on just about everything, but the thoughts of others should never shape your worth. Only God should be the author and sustainer of your identity. John, the author of today's scripture, self-identified as "the disciple Jesus loved." This moniker shaped John's life and thus influenced his ministry after Jesus was gone.

The more you step into your identity as a beloved child of God, the more critical words will slide off your back. When you seek the Lord as the source for everything in your life, there will be no room for others' words to define you.

▶ Reflection

How do others' words affect you? Do you find yourself dwelling on what people say to you, or do you quickly move on?

FEELING
REJECTED

If the world hates you, keep in mind that it hated me first.

John 15:18

One purpose in Jesus coming to this world was to help us find comfort in knowing there is a kinship between ourselves and God. Jesus suffered profoundly, and people rejected Him so greatly that it led to His execution, all because He was who He was. Although Jesus was the way—good, kind, and a source of healing—people hated Him because He told the truth about things that needed to change in people's hearts.

There are many scenarios daily that might lead to rejection. A loved one might turn against us, we may not get the job we apply for, or a friend might pull away. Rejection is part of the human experience; it will happen to us all. But when it happens, we have a choice: to stay for a long time in our hurt or realize that Jesus came so that God would never reject any of us. Yes, some form of rejection will cross our path, but we will never encounter God's rejection, for He will never leave or forsake us.

▸ *Prayer*
Lord, help me tether my security to You and the fact that You will never reject me. When others do reject me, help me remember You never leave my side. Amen.

HELPING SOMEONE IN THEIR STRUGGLES

Carry each other's burdens, and in this way you will fulfill the law of Christ.

Galatians 6:2

We all have people in our lives who sometimes struggle or need help. Yet being Christ's hands and feet to others can feel intimidating. Feeling doubtful or being unsure of what to say or do can stop us from reaching out to others.

If you are ever feeling nudged by God to do something for someone who is hurting or overburdened, stop and talk to Him. Ask Him to provide you with the courage and the actions to help someone in their struggles. It might feel uncomfortable at first, but the more you step out to help others in need, the easier it will become. We may also be unsure of what to say to those in need, but it's not about having the right words. It's about being a light to others while they are burdened. The Lord will lead you. All you have to do is to be open and willing for Him to direct your steps.

▶ Activity

Prayerfully ask God to show you someone you can help today. Ask Him to put that person in your path and give you the confidence to reach out.

MONEY DOESN'T SOLVE YOUR PROBLEMS

Keep your lives free from the love of money and be content with what you have, because God has said, "Never will I leave you; never will I forsake you."

Hebrews 13:5

Jesus, the apostle Paul, and other New Testament authors spoke a lot about money and wealth, often citing it as a distraction, something people tend to worship. Yes, we need money to pay for necessities, but pursuing more wealth or buying more things beyond what we truly need (assuming we have the means to do so) won't guarantee a happy life. God is the only true answer to every problem we face.

There will always be bills that need to be paid. Sometimes we find ourselves stuck in money problems, unexpected expenses, or living beyond our means. When these things happen, it offers us an opportunity to lean on God in new and transformational ways. The Lord will provide what you need. In addition, He calls us to be content with what we have. One way we can help alleviate money woes is by actively pursuing gratitude for how much the Lord has already provided for us.

▶ Prayer

Lord, help me put my trust in You, not my finances. You are the way to true freedom, and I seek only Your support. Please provide for my every need. Amen.

LONGING
FOR THE PAST

He who was seated on the throne said, "I am making everything new!" Then he said, "Write this down, for these words are trustworthy and true."

Revelation 21:5

It is a natural tendency to look to the past and long for the ways things used to be, but looking in the rearview mirror only robs from us what God is doing in the present. God is at work here and now, and He is bringing newness and freshness to your life. But if you are always looking backward, you might miss what God is doing and how He wants to provide for you in the present. God brings to our lives paths we may never even have thought about walking down. There is true fulfillment when we open ourselves up to the presence of God at work in our lives.

Life with God is an adventure, much like it was when Jesus walked with His disciples. You never know what God will bring, but if you are dwelling on the past and wishing things were like they used to be, then you will likely miss the amazing goodness God has in store for you today, tomorrow, and the rest of your life!

▸ Reflection
Do you find yourself longing for how something used to be? If so, what would it be like for you to focus on what God is doing now?

LOOKING TOWARD THE FUTURE

He will wipe every tear from their eyes. There will be no more death or mourning or crying or pain, for the old order of things has passed away.

Revelation 21:4

We conclude this series of devotions with a future promise. The fullness of our relationship with Jesus will be realized in Heaven. There, we will no longer face any suffering, persecution, injustice, pain, sorrow, or death. You see, these conditions are all the result of the broken world we currently reside in. But Jesus came to pave the way for us to have an impactful relationship with Him here in this world while we wait for the next one.

When life is difficult or you feel discontent, it's important to set your eyes on your future reality. In Heaven, with Jesus, you will be fulfilled in ways you never dreamed. While abounding in joy, peace, and love, you will find your home walking hand in hand with Christ. It will be a glorious day!

▶ Reflection
Think about your life without suffering, pain, or loss. Can you envision what your life will be like in Heaven with Jesus?

Grow Your Relationship with Jesus

Congratulations on reaching the end of this devotional! I hope that you walk away from this sacred time with Jesus feeling that you know Him more intimately. Jesus is the answer to every situation we face, and the more you grow your relationship with Him, the stronger and more resilient you become. Life throws a lot of curveballs, and the way we become unshakable is through our ever-growing relationship with Jesus and the growth of His virtues and likeness in our lives.

I hope you take this devotional as a jumping-off point to cultivate more intentional time with Jesus. Adapt some of the exercises in the devotionals, such as journaling, scripture study, and a deeper prayer life, and make them part of your walk with Jesus. These are invaluable tools for every follower of His, as they help us connect to Him and offer opportunities for Him to continue to transform us into His likeness.

About the Author

Alexis Waid holds a master's degree from Denver Seminary, where she focused on practical theology and spiritual formation. Alexis has been doing ministry for twenty years and focuses on the human condition and connecting to God as the source of health, wholeness, guidance, and contentment. She has led countless people online into deeper faith through her website, SpirituallyHungry.com. She is a mother of two kids with special needs and a wife to her best friend and ministry partner, Aaron.

CPSIA information can be obtained
at www.ICGtesting.com
Printed in the USA
LVHW071555140123
737184LV00006B/29

9 781685 396466